Catechism on the Religious State

CATECHISM ON
THE RELIGIOUS STATE

In Conformity with the Code of Canon Law

~~~~~~~~~~~~~~~~~~~~~~~~~~~~~~~~~~~~~~~

BY LOUIS FANFANI, O.P.

Translated by

PAUL C. PERROTTA, O.P.

B. HERDER BOOK CO.

15 & 17 South Broadway. St. Louis 2, Mo.

AND *33 Queen Square, London, W.C.*

This is a translation of *Catechismo Sullo Stato Religioso* by Louis Fanfani, O.P., published at Rome by Marietti, 1946.

IMPRIMI POTEST

> T. S. McDermott, O.P.
> *Provincial*

IMPRIMATUR

> ✠ Joseph E. Ritter, S.T.D.
> *Archbishop of St. Louis*

September 30, 1955

Library of Congress Catalog Card Number: 56-7080

*Printed in the United States of America
by Vail-Ballou Press, Inc., Binghamton, New York*

Author's Preface

THE purpose of this little volume is well defined by its title, "Catechism," for it is intended to guide with the greatest possible brevity and clarity both male and female novices of any religious institute in their immediate preparation for profession. Canon 565 specifically directs that during their year of novitiate, all novices, besides acquiring a knowledge of the rule and constitutions of their particular institute, "should receive instructions on those matters which pertain to the vows and virtues" of the religious state.

There is no lack of books for this purpose, whether for those who should learn or for masters and mistresses who should impart the learning. With rare exceptions, however, most of these books, once they have established soundly the essential notions on the religious life and have indicated with clearness the chief disciplinary ordinances of the Church, launch out heavily into mysticism and asceticism. Without doubt, this is excellent in illuminating and preparing the soul to make a good profession, but it does not fulfill the expressed requirements of the Code which demand the acquisition of clear and precise notions on what the religious life is in itself, apart from the particular rules of the institute in which one is to make profession. This *Catechism on the Religious State* aims precisely to supply so obvious a need.

There is nothing new or strange in this little volume. It is but a compact collection, in question-answer form, of the principal theological and canonical notions concerning the religious life. Its purpose is to help all novices prepare themselves for the customary examination which is conducted in all institutes shortly before they are admitted to profession, and to inspire them with fervor so that they may continue to fulfill the obligations of the life assumed. It is my firm conviction that in many cases the lack of zeal to be good religious stems precisely from the fact that novices were not given clear notions as to what actually constitutes the religious state in the mind of the Church as she conceives it in the light of the Gospels and as she indicates it through her theology and law.

The exposition of the fundamental laws governing the religious life may be found a little dry. Therefore, I have thought it suitable as an appeal to fervor of spirit indispensable for the faithful and fruitful observance of these very laws, to add in the appendix the "Brief Dialogue on Consummate Perfection" written by Saint Catherine of Siena. This little work of hers, in my judgment, is most efficacious to enkindle in the soul of the novice from the very beginning a luminous concept of and a blazing desire for religious perfection.

May the Savior bless these purposes.

LOUIS FANFANI, O.P.

TRANSLATOR'S NOTE

FOR the purpose of this translation, Father Fanfani brought the work up to date, so that in this English version the reader will find several notes and recent decisions not found in the original Italian.

Contents

Catechism on the Religious State

Chapter 1

~~~~~~~~~~~~~~~~~~~~~~~~~~~~~~~~~~~~~

The Religious State

~~~~~~~~~~~~~~~~~~~~~~~~~~~~~~~~~~~~~

Q. 1. What is meant by the religious state?

A. The religious state is thus defined in the Code of Canon Law: "A permanent mode of living in common, by which the faithful, besides obeying the commandments, also observe the evangelical counsels embodied in the vows of obedience, chastity, and poverty" (can. 487).

Q. 2. What, then, in the juridical concept of the Church, are the essential elements that constitute the religious state?

A. The essential elements are three:

1. The practice of evangelical perfection;

2. The taking of the three vows of poverty, chastity, and obedience;

3. The living, permanently and in common, of a certain form of life.

Whatever in the past may have been the opinion of theologians and of canonists with reference to the "living in common" as an essential element of the religious state, today, in the juridical concept of the Church, there is no true religious state without some form of common life. But it may be asked: Is the actual dwelling in the same house, or, as they say, under the same roof, absolutely indispensable for this? Before the

issuance of the constitution, *Provida Mater Ecclesia,* by Pope
Pius XII on February 2, 1947, a doubt was entertainable. Before that time one could hold that the practice of the same
daily observances in the keeping of the same common rule
under the eye and authoritative control of the superiors of
the institute were elements sufficient to constitute, really and
juridically, a certain form of life in common. But after the
publication of the above-mentioned constitution, it seems to
us that there is no longer room for any doubt. To have a common life it must be lived under the same roof, that is, as it
ordinarily unfolds in the same house. Indeed, in the aforesaid
constitution there is given among other things, as a distinction between secular institutes and religious institutes, that
true religious institutes require the habitual dwelling of its
members under the same roof, whereas this is neither had nor
demanded by secular institutes.

Q. 3. Why is this form of religious life called a state?
A. Because the word, state, from the Latin root, *stare,* means,
in its reference to human life, that particular manner of life
which makes stable and permanent the duties and circumstances of living on the part of the person who embraces it.
Now the religious life, as we have said above, is a precise form
of life in which the faithful who embrace it oblige themselves
to practice permanently and perseveringly not only the ordinary precepts but the evangelical counsels as well. Thus
they enter into a specialized field of spiritual living which
changes radically and lastingly the modes of the common Christian life. Therefore, the religious life is truly and properly a
state.[1]

Q. 4. Why is this state called religious?
A. Because it demands of him who embraces it the total consecration of self to the worship and service of God. In it, one's
whole life and all his actions become a continuous homage

[1] *Summa theol.,* IIa–IIae, q. 183, a. 1.

rendered to the sovereign excellence of God. Since any form
of worship pertains to that great moral virtue called religion,
this most excellent and stable form of worship is properly
entitled the religious state.

Q. 5. In reference to Christian living, how many are the principal states of life?

A. The principal states of Christian life are four, namely:

1. The ecclesiastical state, which comprises the diocesan
clergy;

2. The religious state, which embraces all religious;

3. The conjugal state, which refers to all married persons;

4. The celibate state, which includes all those who voluntarily remain unmarried in the world.

Q. 6. Which one of these states is the most perfect?

A. It is of faith, defined by the Council of Trent,[2] that even
simple voluntary celibacy in the world practiced out of love for
our Lord Jesus Christ is more perfect, considered in itself, than
the conjugal state. As a consequence, the ecclesiastical and religious states, in which one voluntarily practices celibacy, also
are more perfect than the conjugal state. Furthermore, since
the religious state imposes the practice not only of perfect
chastity but also of the other evangelical counsels, namely,
poverty and obedience, we must conclude that the religious
state is evidently more perfect than simple voluntary celibacy
in the world.

If we restrict the question exclusively to an evaluation of
the religious state and the ecclesiastical state, we hold that the
ecclesiastical state, from the standpoint of authority and
dignity, is definitely superior to the religious state. The order
of priesthood, indeed, imparts to him who receives it so man-
datory a power over souls that no other order in the world
equals it. If, however, we are speaking of spiritual perfection,
it seems we must conclude that the religious state in itself is

[2] Sess. XXIV, on the sacrament of matrimony.

more perfect than the ecclesiastical state. This is because by taking the vows of poverty, chastity, and obedience in the religious state one has the better means of tending to perfection. Besides, in this particular state, one is obliged more strictly and more explicitly to tend to perfection.[3]

Objectively considered the religious state, therefore, is more perfect than any other. Justly, then, the Code directs that this state "is to be honored by all" (can. 487).

In practice, of course, each Catholic must embrace that state to which he feels called by God. By faithful compliance with the duties of his particular vocation, each man can attain his perfection in God's sight.

Q. 7. If the religious state is so excellent, why was it, and why is it still, the most persecuted of all the various institutions of the Church?

A. Precisely because it is excellent. Whoever is an enemy of our Lord Jesus Christ is also an enemy of His Church, and, by consequence, of the various excellent institutions fostered by the Church. Indeed, he is the more inimical in ratio to the greater excellence of the institution. The religious orders always have labored prodigiously to achieve the highest purposes in the mind of the Church—the supernatural life and the seeking of perfection—while they have been, and still are, of the greatest utility in her work of saving souls. What wonder is it, then, that the enemy of goodness has nearly always taken issue and continues to take issue with the religious orders?

Q. 8. Why does the religious state exist in the Church under various forms? In other words, why are there so many religious orders so different and distinct among themselves?

A. We can assign many reasons, but the most obvious one surely is that the Savior wills to preserve the greatest freedom

3 *Summa theol.,* IIa–IIae, q. 184, a. 8.

for souls both in the choice of a state and in the practical exercise of the duties which devolve upon each from the choice. Wherefore, we see a providential flowering of multiple religious institutions in the Church, particularly of the great religious orders, for in them each one who is called can pursue his religious vocation in that mode which best corresponds to his needs and desires. Besides, the Church herself shines the more resplendently the more varied and numerous are the forms of activity in which her religious engage.

Q. *9.* Who founded the religious state?
A. The religious state, considered in its nature and in its supreme purpose, was established by our Lord Jesus Christ. In its practical actualization throughout the centuries it has been regulated and organized by the Church, which has done nothing more than give a concrete form to that kind of life which Jesus Christ Himself had already established through His recommendation of the evangelical counsels.

Therefore, the origin of the religious life is not due to the saintly founders of religious institutes. These determined only the forms in which they desired their followers to practice the life of perfection in the religious state founded by our Lord Himself.

Q. *10.* To what is the religious obliged by reason of his state?
A. By reason of his state, the religious is obliged to tend constantly and with all his powers to evangelical perfection (can. 593).

Q. *11.* In what does evangelical perfection consist?
A. Evangelical perfection consists in the practice of perfect charity. This greatest of all virtues has the power within it of excluding from the soul all that which is contrary to the love of God, namely, any leaning towards sin, while it includes a positive desire to practice all those forms of goodness which, going

beyond those of strict obligation, enter into the realm of pure love and aid the soul in turning with all its powers to God.[4]

It is called evangelical precisely because the Gospels themselves speak of this degree of absolute perfection. It is in the Gospel that Jesus invites us to its practice with these words: "If thou wilt be perfect, go sell what thou hast, and give to the poor . . . and come, follow Me" (Matt. 12, 21).

Q. 12. What is meant, then, by the obligation in the religious state "to tend to perfection"?
A. It does not mean that he who embraces this state need be already perfect, but that he must will to exert himself to become so. If a religious is not serious about acquiring perfection, he fails positively in one of the fundamental duties, indeed in the first duty, of his state.[5]

Q. 13. By what means should the religious tend to perfection?
A. By the observance of:
   1. The three vows of poverty, chastity, and obedience, as principal and indispensable means (can. 488, 1);
   2. The prescriptions of the rule, as subsidiary means (same canon);
   3. Every other virtue, obligatory or not, which can increase charity in himself, which is the love of God and union with God.[6]

Q. 14. Why are the three vows of poverty, chastity, and obedience the principal and indispensable means of tending to perfection?
A. Because our Lord Jesus Christ so taught. To the young man who asked Him what he should do to be perfect, Jesus replied: "Go, sell what thou hast and give to the poor, and thou shalt have treasure in heaven; and come follow Me"

---

[4] *Summa theol.,* IIa–IIae. q. 184, a. 2.
[5] *Summa theol.,* IIa–IIae, q. 184, a. 3.
[6] *Summa theol.,* IIa–IIae, q. 186, a. 3.

(Matt. 19, 21). In this passage we have manifest evidence of the counsel of voluntary poverty.

To the apostles who asked Jesus if it were expedient to marry or not, He replied praising perfect chastity as a privileged grace. "All men take not this word, but they to whom it is given. . . . He that can take, let him take it" (Matt. 19, 11–12).

Finally, as a means of great perfection, Jesus recommended the virtue of self-denial. "If any man will come after Me, let him deny himself, and take up his cross, and follow Me" (Matt. 16, 24). This text obviously recommends the virtue of obedience.

Q. 15. Are there other reasons to show that these three vows are efficacious means to perfection?

A. Yes, there are. In the first place, there is the experience of daily life. When we realize the effects of original sin in the cravings of the human heart for the things of earth, for the gratification of the senses, and for indulgence in pride, we see that the three greatest obstacles to perfection are removed by the three vows. The vow of poverty opposes the inordinate greed for material goods; the vow of chastity strengthens the soul against the surges of lust, while the vow of obedience attacks self-love and all the consequences which result from this inborn inclination to independence.

Secondly, the very taking of the vows is itself one of the greatest acts of perfection. Religious profession is an act of offering, indeed of sacrifice, to God of all the desirable goods which man possesses in this world: the goods of fortune by the vow of poverty, the personal goods of the body by the vow of chastity, and the intimate goods of the soul by the vow of obedience. Sacrifice, we know, is the highest act of the virtue of religion.

Thus are the three vows efficacious, indeed, essential, means of tending to perfection in the religious life. So essential are they that without them there is no religious state according to the mind and laws of the Church (can. 487).

Q. *16.* How does the rule become a means for the practicing of perfection?

A. Because it helps in the observance of the aforesaid vows, indicating their particular obligations and affording protections against the dangers to which the vows are exposed in practical living. Besides, for the purposes of perfection, the rule serves all the other virtues in accordance with the aims and spirit of each religious institute.

From this it is apparent that the observance of the rule is a practical and continual exercise of perfection. Its definite injunctions are more efficacious and trustworthy than a spirit of simple observance of the vows or of simple diligence in avoiding sin.

Q. *17.* When does the religious sin against his obligation of tending to perfection?

A. The religious sins against his obligation of tending to perfection when he transgresses his vows and when he positively withdraws his will from the practice of virtue and advancement in perfection.

Q. *18.* Is it possible for a religious to be so perverse as to consent to such a withdrawal of will?

A. A positive and formal withdrawal of his will from the practice of virtue is hard to conceive in a religious; it is most rare if found at all. But there can be found an equivalent withdrawal of will in the deplorable case when a religious consents to trespass habitually and contemptuously against the rules of his state.

Q. *19.* On the contrary, what is the quality of the deportment of a religious who with his whole heart tends to perfection?

A. A religious who is truly tending to perfection in exact observance of his vows and constitutions is all charity, his charity extending to all in equal measure. He is patient under buffetings, docile under reproofs, candid in soul, discreet in word, an enemy of ease, assiduous in prayer. He disdains all things which savor of the world, he crushes under foot all human respect, and with resolute spirit marches steadfast in the teachings and examples of our Lord Jesus Christ along the path to paradise.

Q. *20.* How does a religious fire himself with zeal to keep working with all his strength for his own perfection?

A. The religious fires himself with zeal to keep working for perfection by keeping always before his eyes the high purpose for which he entered religion, and by reminding himself that he who is not thoroughly determined to advance along the road to perfection actually retreats, thus running the risk of being lost eternally. "Not to advance is to retreat," is the solemn warning of the great St. Augustine.

Q. *21.* What particular benefits does the religious state bring to man?

A. "In religion," says St. Bernard, "man lives a life more pure and more pleasing to God; he falls less frequently, he rises from a fall more quickly, he advances with more caution, is endowed more abundantly with divine graces and enjoys a permanent peace. He dies with greater confidence in God's mercy, he is more promptly released from purgatory, and is rewarded more generously in heaven." [7]

[7] From the homily, *Simile Est Regnum Coelorum.*

~~~~~~

Chapter 2

The Different Kinds of
Religious Institutes

~~~~~~

Q. 22. What is a religious institute?

A. A religious institute, or more simply, religion, in the sense in which we are presently treating it, is: "A society approved by legitimate ecclesiastical authority, whose members strive after evangelical perfection by observing the special laws of that society and by making public vows, either perpetual or temporary, the latter to be renewed when the time expires" (can. 488, 1).

Q. 23. Why is the approval of the Church required in order to have a religious institute?

A. Because it belongs to the Church to judge whether or not a form of religious life is really good and conforms to the spirit of the Gospel; also, because the establishing of the various religious associations enters within the domain of her hierarchical power whereby she has the right and duty to provide and preserve organizations among the faithful; finally, because the Church has the obligation to confirm the rights and duties which the faithful, either as individuals or as societies, have as members within the very bosom of herself, the perfect society.

There is a dispute among the doctors as to whether or not it is absolutely necessary for the Church to approve an organization before it can be considered a true religious state and a religion strictly so called. Is the approval of the Church by its very nature an essential element for the having of a religious institute? This question has not been decided. However, this much is certain: According to the present legislation of the Church, no association can claim the dignity of a true religious institute unless it has secured the approval of the competent ecclesiastical authority. This is clearly the tenor of canon 488, 1.

Q. 24. How many kinds of religious institutes may there be?
A. Religious institutes, for men and women, are classified:

1. By reason of their vows, into orders and religious congregations. A religious order is that society in which solemn vows are taken by virtue of the rule, while a religious congregation is a society wherein only simple vows, perpetual or temporary, are taken (can. 488, 2).[8]

2. By reason of its approbation, a religious institute is either of papal law or of diocesan law. An institute of papal law is that which has obtained from the Holy See itself direct approval, or at least the *decretum laudis,* the decree of praise, while of diocesan law is that society which has been approved by the ordinary of the place but which as yet has not obtained

---

[8] "By virtue of the rule," that is, as provided for by the rule and proper constitutions of each institute. It is not necessary in order to have a religious order that all the members take solemn vows: it is enough that at least some of them can and must take them.

Up to the sixteenth century only religious orders existed in the Church. It was in that century that new institutes for men and women originated whose members took only simple vows and so there came into being the religious congregations, so called, to distinguish them from the religious orders properly speaking. Later the pious societies or religious congregations without vows came into being and, very recently, secular institutes have been approved.

even a decree of praise from the Holy See (can. 488, 3).[9]

3. By reason of jurisdiction a religious institute is either exempt or nonexempt. That institute of solemn or even of simple vows is exempt which has been removed, except in those cases expressly mentioned in common law, from the jurisdiction of the ordinary of the place; while non-exempt institutes are those which are subject in all things to the jurisdiction of the ordinary of the place, as are the simple faithful and the diocesan clergy (can. 488, 2 and 615).[10]

4. By reason of ministry a religious institute is either clerical or lay. Those institutes are clerical whose members, in good number at least, are priests; lay institutes are those whose members are not by rule promoted to the priesthood. Even though some of the members, by way of exception or by virtue of a dispensation, are priests, the lay character of the institute remains according to the rule (can. 488, 4).[11]

[9] The Holy See in approving religious institutes follows the practice of granting first the so-called decree of praise, in which are cited as meritorious the good intentions of the founder, the aims of the institute, and the fruits already realized, without entering into the merits of the institute or having at present the intention to approve it. It is only after many renewed requests on the part of those interested, and upon evidence of a definite utility for the Church and for souls that the Holy See concedes its approbation to a new religious institute.

It is well to note that a religious congregation of diocesan law, even though in the course of time it may spread out into many dioceses, as long as it has not obtained papal approval or at least the decree of praise, always remains under diocesan jurisdiction, fully subject to the authority of the ordinary (can. 492, 2; and New Norms, etc., of the Sacred Congregation of Religious, c. 1, n. 5).

[10] Therefore, not only the institutes with solemn vows, but also those with simple vows can enjoy, more or less amply, the privilege of exemption, if and just as it may please the Holy Father.

[11] Female religious institutes are necessarily and in every instance lay in character. Male institutes, on the contrary, can be either lay or clerical, according to the aims and dispositions of their proper rule. The Benedictines, Franciscans, Dominicans, etc., are clerical because many of their members, indeed we may say the majority of them, are raised to the priesthood. The Do Good Brothers of Saint John of God, the Christian Brothers of Saint Jean Baptist de la Salle, etc., even if there may be found among them a priest or two, are lay institutes, because their members are by their rule destined to remain in the lay state.

5. By reason of the kind of life lived in them, institutes may be contemplative, active, or mixed.

Contemplative institutes are those in which the members principally apply themselves, under one form or another, to prayer and contemplation.

Active institutes are those which have as their proper and principal aim the practice of some work of mercy for the good of the neighbor, such as preaching, the education of the young, the care of the sick, and so forth.

Mixed institutes are those which by rule dedicate themselves both to contemplation and to action, not indeed as two separate things one after the other, but rather as two things which fuse and strengthen each other, the external action being sparked by contemplation while contemplation itself takes on new life and vigor from the action. An example of this is the Dominican Order, in which the preaching apostolate is fused with the choral recitation of the office and other monastic observances.

Q. 25. Is the religious contemplative life more perfect than the active?

A. To this question, St. Thomas Aquinas thus replies:

1. Taken in itself the contemplative life is without doubt more perfect than the active life, inasmuch as the contemplative life has as its immediate object God Himself, while the active life arrives at God by way of the neighbor. Actions which aim directly at God are certainly more perfect than those which aim at Him indirectly by way of another.

2. In particular cases, however, having in mind the necessities of the present life, there can be given circumstances in which the active life is more perfect than the contemplative life.

3. Over and above these two the mixed life is to be preferred.

His reason for this conclusion is contained in a memorable passage in the *Summa:* [12]

[12] *Summa theol.,* IIa–IIae, q. 188, a. 6.

As it is more perfect to illuminate than merely to shine, so is it more perfect to give unto others the fruits of our contemplation than to hoard them for self alone.

Our Blessed Lord and the apostles lived this kind of mixed life; hence, obviously, it is the best kind of religious living.

Q. 26. What is meant by pious religious societies and pious religious congregations?

A. Pious religious societies and congregations are associations of persons living in common, in the manner of religious under the direction of definite superiors, and in conformity with constitutions regularly approved, but who do not bind themselves to the usual three public vows (can. 673, 1).

For a vow to be "public" it must be accepted by a legitimate ecclesiastical superior in the name of the Church (can. 1308, 1). There is no prohibition against the private taking of the three vows. Frequently, indeed, and laudably, the members of such associations do take them; but these are private vows such as can be taken by any of the faithful by themselves (see note in answer to Q. 124).

Such associations, therefore, do not properly constitute what is canonically known as a religion, nor can the members of these associations, strictly speaking, call themselves religious (can. 673, 1). The reason for this is that they lack one of the three essential elements mentioned above in reply to Questions 2 and 23, namely, the public taking of the three vows with the authorization of the Church and accepted by her.

Q. 27. What are secular institutes?

A. Secular institutes are those societies, clerical or lay, of recent foundation and approbation, whose members, moved by a desire for Christian perfection and with apostolic zeal, make profession of the evangelical counsels while remaining in the world (Constitution, "Provida Mater Ecclesia," February 2, 1947).

The term, "they make profession," here means that without

taking vows they practice the evangelical counsels, particularly the counsel of perfect chastity. For this reason persons who are married are excluded from membership in these secular institutes.

The sentiment, "moved by a desire for Christian perfection," as we said above, is obligatory for religious men and women properly speaking, but it may equally animate persons whose vocation it is to live in the world.

The phrase, "apostolic zeal," requires some form of apostolic activity; wherefore secular institutes dedicated entirely to contemplative living cannot be founded.

"While remaining in the world" means that they live without wearing a definite kind of habit and without obligation to dwell, at least in the ordinary way, in community.

Q. *28.* What is meant by a religious house?
A. A religious house, materially speaking, is a place wherein several members of the same religious institute habitually dwell. Formally, it is the union of several members of the same religious institute who dwell together in community.

It can have various names: abbey, hermitage, convent, monastery, college, oratory, and so on.

Q. *29.* How many kinds of religious houses are there?
A. A religious house, for men or women, can be:

  1. Either formed or nonformed. It is formed if there dwell together at least six professed religious, and if it be a clerical religion, four of them at least are priests (can. 488, 5). It is nonformed if the professed religious who are habitually assigned thereto are less than six.[13]

  2. Either self-governing or not self-governing. It is self-governing when it is independent of other houses or of other

---

[13] Since the Code uses the word "professed," we cannot count among the required number of six for a formed house any novice, much less a postulant. We may, however, for this purpose, count one who is professed of simple vows even though the institute is of solemn vows.

superiors outside of those dwelling in that house. In other words, it is a house that manages itself. It is not self-governing when the members and its own local superiors are responsible to other superiors of the institute, for example, a provincial or general.

3. Whether from a legal or historic standpoint, according to grade, a religious house can be a motherhouse, a principal house, or a filial house.

The motherhouse, in the historic sense, is the house of origin, the place where the order or congregation sprang into being. In the legal sense, a motherhouse is the house where the superior general habitually resides. For this reason it may be called also the *casa generalizia,* the general's house or generalate and *curia generalizia,* the general's chancery.

The principal house is that house which has under it as offspring or branches one or more small houses which do not enjoy a legal personality but which depend upon this principal house.

A filial house is that house which is not autonomous even in its local functioning, but depends on another house which governs it. A filial house, therefore, has these characteristics:

1. It is not a moral person distinct from the principal house;

2. It does not have its own chapter or council, but its members form part, if they have the proper qualifications, of the chapter and council of the principal house;

3. It does not possess any goods of its own, these, if there be any, belonging to the principal house;

4. It can have its own superior, who, however, has no personal authority but only the authority delegated by the superior of the principal house;

5. It is truly a religious house, even though it is but filial in status (cf., Sacred Congregation of Religious, February 1, 1924). For this reason for its erection and its functioning there are demanded the same conditions required for the erection and the operation of any religious house.

Chapter 3

The Different Kinds
of Religious

Q. *30.* Who are religious?

A. In the present-day legislation of the Church religious are those persons who take vows in a religious institute (can. 488, 7).

While it is true that all those who honor God are commonly known as religious people or religious, as St. Thomas notes in his *Summa theol.* (IIa–IIae, q. 86, a. 1, ad 5m), strictly and specifically only those who consecrate their lives to God's service are to be named religious, for these, by the taking of vows, separate themselves as far as is possible from the affairs of the world. As they who merely contemplate are not said to be contemplatives, since this title fits only those who make of contemplation their life's work, so they who are religious-minded are not said to be religious, for this name applies only to those who make of religion their life's consecration.

Q. *31.* What are the different kinds of religious?

A. Religious persons are differentiated naturally first as religious men or women. From this primary differentiation others ensue:

1. Religious men who are either regulars or religious of simple vows. Regulars are those religious who take their vows in an order, that is, they take solemn vows (can. 488, 7). They are called mendicants if their rule obliges or permits them to solicit alms for their sustenance. They are nonmendicants if their honest living is provided for by goods possessed in common (can. 621, 1).[14] On the other hand, religious of simple vows are those who take vows in a religious congregation. They are not called regulars, but, simply, religious (can. 488, 7). In these congregations the vows, even if they are perpetual, are always simple.

2. Religious women are either nuns or sisters. Nuns, strictly, are female religious who take solemn vows; for example, the Benedictines, cloistered Dominicans, and so on. This includes female religious who, although by their rule should take solemn vows, by dispensation of the Holy See for certain regions, take only simple vows. These religious, except where the very nature of the case or the clear content of the law imposes the contrary, are to be classified as nuns in the strict sense (can. 488, 7).

Sisters, in the canonical sense of the word, are female religious who take simple vows. They take vows in an institute wherein only simple vows are permitted and prescribed by rule, even if they are perpetual (can. 488, 7).

Therefore, although the titles "nuns" and "sisters" frequently are interchanged or confused in ordinary conversation, by law of the Church these titles stand for distinct categories among persons. "Religious" is a name which fits both nuns and sisters as a common genus, while the title, "nun," is a specific one fitting only a special class of religious women.

It follows, then, that whatever in the legislation of the Church is said concerning religious women, applies equally

14 "In common," which means, therefore, that no regular may privately own any property or material goods. Such ownership is forbidden because it is contrary to the very nature of the solemn vow of poverty (see Q. 156). This prohibition applies to nonmendicants as well as to mendicants.

to nuns and sisters; but what is said concerning sisters does not apply to nuns, and what is said concerning nuns does not apply to sisters, excepting a case wherein the legislator clearly indicates that what is said of one applies to the other.

Chapter 4

The Government of Religious

Q. 32. By whom are religious governed?

A. Religious are governed by:

1. The pope, both in his capacity as supreme head of all the faithful and as first superior of all religious by virtue of their vow of obedience (can. 495, 1).

2. The Sacred Congregation of Religious, since this is the immediate body deputized by the Holy Father to govern religious (can. 251).

3. The ordinary of the place, unless by special privilege religious are exempt from his jurisdiction, and then only to the extent of the exemption (can. 500, 1).

4. The proper superiors of the institute of which the religious are members (can. 500, 1).

Q. 33. Is the cardinal protector of the orders and religious congregations a true superior?

A. The cardinal protector of an order or of a religious congregation is not a true and proper superior. He is rather a patron, since the pope confides to him, at the request of the religious institute, the care of, or better, the particular help to the institute of which he has been named the protector before the Roman Curia (can. 499, 2).

Although the cardinal protector is not a true and proper superior, the practice of the Roman Curia, however, has introduced the usage that he can make, in place of the ordinary, the so-called *commendatizia,* or the "I sponsor the petition," in the pleas which the religious present to the Holy See for dispensations, indults, and so on; and the Sacred Congregation generally transmits to the cardinal protector the so-called executive orders when it concedes the dispensation or indult.

Q.   34. Who is the ordinary of the place?
A. The ordinary of the place is the bishop of the diocese, or whoever in the diocese acts for or as the bishop, whether he be an abbot, a prelate *nullius,* an apostolic administrator, a vicar apostolic, a prefect apostolic, and so on. The vicar general and the vicar capitular of a diocese also come under the name of the ordinary of the place (can. 198, 1).

Therefore, the title, ordinary of the place, has a meaning somewhat different from that of bishop of the place, inasmuch as one can be the ordinary of the place without being a bishop, as in the case of the prefect apostolic. When there is no need to make the distinction, the title bishop or ordinary may be used to indicate the superior of the diocese.

Q.   35. Who, for religious, is the ordinary of the place?
A. For religious of either sex the ordinary of the place is the ordinary of the diocese wherein the monastery or convent in question is located, or wherein the religious men or women are assigned (can. 965).

Q.   36. Who is the proper pastor of the religious?
A. The proper pastor of religious men or women—in those things which come under his competence—is the pastor of the parish wherein is located the convent or monastery to which the religious belong (can. 1221, 1 and 1230, 5).

Q.   37. Who are the proper superiors of a religious institute?

A. The proper superiors of a religious institute are the superiors appointed or elected by the members of the institute. They are called "proper" to distinguish them from other superiors which the institute may have outside its own membership, as in the case of the ordinary or when a regular is named superior over several monasteries of nuns.

Q. 38. What title is given to these proper superiors?
A. The superiors of a religious institute have various names according to the provision of each institute and the particular office enjoyed. Thus the local superior in some male institutes is called the guardian; in others, the prior, or president, or minister; while in some others simply the superior. The provincial superior is sometimes called the provincial, at other times the visitator, and so on. There is no one title designating the supreme office in all institutes, each institute preferring to call its head by a title peculiar to itself. Commonly, however, the title of superior general covers the situation. The same may be said of female institutes.

Q. 39. According to the Code how are the proper superiors of a religious institute classified?
A. They are classified as major and minor (can. 488, 8).

Q. 40. Who are the major superiors?
A. The major superiors are:

1. the superior general of the institute, whatever may be his particular title, such as primatial abbot, abbot, superior abbot of an independent monastery, master general, minister general, and so on; likewise, their vicars and visitators;

2. the provincial superiors, together with their vicars, and all those who under the title of visitators, assistants, and so on, exercise an authority over the subjects like that of a provincial (can. 488, 8);

3. in female institutes the abbess, the superior of an inde-

pendent monastery, or the mother general, with their vicars, are major superiors.

Q. 41. Who are the minor superiors?
A. The minor superiors are all the other superiors inferior in grade to the major superiors.

Q. 42. What requisites, according to Canon Law, must a religious possess to be a major superior?
A. According to canon 504, which begins by confirming all the other requirements of age and condition laid down by the constitutions of each religious body, the following are the minimum requisites for the office of major superior:

1. That the religious has completed at least ten years of profession in the same religion in which he now finds himself, the time being computed from his first profession therein;

2. That he has been born of lawful wedlock. This requirement is cancelled if subsequently he has become legitimate through the marriage of his parents (can. 1117).

3. That he be at least thirty years of age, which holds even for provincials. However, for the office of highest superior in the institute, or for a superior in a monastery of nuns, one must have completed forty years of age.

Q. 43. What requirements are laid down by the Code for minor superiors?
A. None in particular. Therefore, it is sufficient that the religious appointed or elected to a minor office have the legal qualifications demanded by the constitutions of his own institute and by the very nature of the office which he is called upon to fill. However, in the case of nuns, as stated above, even the local superior, whether or not she is regarded as a major superior, has to be at least forty years of age (can. 504).

Q. 44. Are the proper superiors of religious to govern for life or for a specified period?

A. Minor superiors are to govern only for a specified period (can. 505). Major superiors may hold tenure for life if their legitimately approved constitutions allow it (*ibid.*).

Q. 45. How long may a minor superior remain in office?
A. A local superior should not remain in office more than three years. However, having finished this three-year term, he can be elected or appointed a second time, thus succeeding himself, if his constitutions allow it. However, he cannot be named for a third term in the same house unless there has been an interval in his tenure between the second and third term (can. 505).

The three-year term is computed according to the calendar (can. 34, 3). The term expires at the end of the day of the third year after his installation. Thus, if the term had begun March 1, 1953, it expires at the end of the day of March 1, 1956, even in leap years.

"In the same house" means that the same religious cannot succeed himself more than once in that house; but if he passes to another house he can be elected or appointed to the same office therein.

As to the interval between the second and third term, the Code does not say how long this has to be. It leaves the determination of it to the constitutions.

"If the constitutions allow it" means that even though the Code permits a second successive term, that is, a third term, it is only on the condition that the constitutions do not forbid it.

In the monasteries of nuns, likewise, the superior cannot remain in office more than three years. As to the possibility of her being renamed after the first term, the constitutions are to be followed (Circular Letter of the Sacred Congregation of Religious to Diocesan Ordinaries, March 9, 1920).

Q. 46. Should the fixed limits of a three-year term for minor superiors be applied equally to those superiors who are at the same time directors of schools, colleges, hospitals, and so on?

A. Yes, the limit of a three-year term applies to those as well if these directors are at the same time superiors of religious in reference to regular discipline (Pontifical Commission for the Interpretation of the Code, June 2–3, 1918).

In other words, if there is a school, a hospice, a hospital, or the like, attached to a religious house, the management and internal discipline of which depend on one local superior, this superior must abide by the law of the three-year term. But if, as often happens, there are two superiors, one called the religious superior, whose concern is the religious discipline of the members according to rule and constitutions, the other called the administrator of the institution, such as a president, principal, director, or the like, whose chief concern is to manage the affairs of the nonreligious patrons of the institution, there is a diversity of procedure. The law of the three-year term applies to the religious superior but not to the superior who is only administrator. The president, principal, director, etc., of an institution, who is not at the same time the religious superior, may carry on for any length of time at the pleasure of his major superior.

Q. 47. What is the length of tenure of office for major superiors when it is by term?

A. The determination of the tenure in this case, whether for three, four, five, six, or more years, rests freely with each religious institute. Nothing on this point is fixed by the Code. It is understood, however, that once the constitutions have been approved by the competent authority—the Holy See for institutes of papal law, the ordinary for institutes of diocesan law—it is not permissible, even on this point, to make changes without a new approval from the institute's immediate superior, namely, the pope for papal institutes, the bishop for diocesan institutes.

Chapter 5

~~~~~~

The Laws That Bind Religious

~~~~~~

Q. 48. By what laws are religious governed?

A. Before all others, religious are subject to the laws and prescriptions already contained in the Code of Canon Law, and to those which in the future may emanate from the Holy See. This is true whether the prescriptions directly concern them, as when issued precisely for the religious, or, when directed to the simple faithful, they can be brought consonantly into religious life. The first and highest superior of all the faithful in the Church, that is, of all religious, ecclesiastics, and laypeople, is always the Supreme Pontiff. By entrance into religion one does not cease to be a Christian or a Catholic. Wherefore, religious are obliged to the observance of those common laws of the Church insofar as they are not contrary to the new state which the Church has allowed them to embrace.

Q. 49. Do diocesan laws oblige the religious?

A. Diocesan laws and prescriptions do oblige the religious who find themselves in the territory of the diocese, as long as they are not exempt (see Q. 24, 3). As we said above, in embracing the religious state, the religious do not cease to be members of the Church, for which reason they continue to be subject to the lawful superiors of the Church in all those things not contrary to their new state.

Q. 50. What other laws, after these, must religious observe?
A. They must observe the rule and constitutions of their particular institute (can. 489).

Q. 51. What is the difference between rule and constitution?
A. The rule, properly speaking, is an ensemble of the fundamental statutes drawn up by the founder or by others, fixing the proper objective of the institute and the principal means of reaching it. The constitution comprises all the definite legislation drawn up and approved for the practical activation of the rule according to the circumstances of time, place, personnel, and the like.

Particularly in the religious congregations of recent origin which hardly ever have their rule distinct from the constitution, it is common to employ either term indifferently to mean the same thing, namely, the proper laws of the institute. However, the Sacred Congregation of Religious in the norms cited above in Q. 45 insists that the proper laws of the religious congregation be simply called constitutions and that the title of rule be given only to the old rules of the religious orders (c. IV, n. 22h).

Q. 52. What are the principal and the oldest rules approved by the Church?
A. The principal and oldest rules approved by the Church are four: that of St. Basil, of St. Augustine, of St. Benedict, and of St. Francis of Assisi.

Q. 53. What are customs?
A. Customs are usages legitimately and praiseworthily introduced, which after a certain passage of time acquire the force of law.

Q. 54. When may a custom be said to be "laudably introduced" in a religious institute?

A. A custom is said to be laudably introduced when it has a good purpose and contributes to the welfare of the community.

Consequently, the following customs are not laudable:

1. those which are contrary to the proper objective of the institute and to regular observance;

2. those which have been expressly revoked by the superior or by law (can. 27, 2);

3. those which are in contradiction with divine law or natural law (can. 27, 1).

Q. 55. When do customs become legitimate?

A. When they are introduced with all those guarantees and conditions which the law requires, particularly with reference to their age.

Q. 56. How much time must pass before a custom becomes legitimate and has the force of law?

A. Customs contrary to the common law of the Church cannot possess the force of law unless they have been in practice for forty full and continuous years, that is to say, they must be able to be traced back forty years without interruption. But if the law which they contravene expressly forbids a contrary custom, a hundred years are required, or even time immemorial (can. 27, 1). For all other customs, only thirty years generally are required.

Q. 57. What is meant by the precepts of superiors?

A. By the precepts of superiors are meant their commands, especially when imposed on single individuals in virtue of the vow of obedience.

Taken in this sense of true command, the precept is distinct from an ordination of the superiors. In the proper sense of the word, ordinations are prescriptions which the superior, in virtue of his office as superior, imposes on his community for observance during the period of his tenure in office in the manner of a rule or a constitution; and these have force, that is, they bind in conscience precisely in the mode by which the constitutions bind. The precept, on the contrary, properly speaking, is a genuine command given to one or more of the subjects in applying the constitutions, or at least conformable to them directly or indirectly, the superior thereby intending to make himself obeyed by his subject or subjects in that precise point indicated by his direct command.

Q. 58. Do the precepts of superiors oblige in conscience?
A. They certainly do (can. 501, 1). To what avail would be the power of the superiors if they, in the regular government of a religious institute or in particular cases and for the good of each member, are incapable of giving an order which obliges the subject (see Q. 235)?

Q. 59. What is meant by a formal precept?
A. A formal precept is an expressed command of the superior given precisely in virtue of holy obedience and under grave penalty.

Q. 60. Does he who disobeys a formal precept commit a mortal sin?
A. Certainly, if he does it with full consciousness and deliberate will. It is required, however, that the precept be given in the precise manner which the laws and proper constitutions specify (Q. 227 and others which follow).

Chapter 6

Conditions for Admission into a Religious Institute

Q. *61.* What conditions are required for admission into a religious institute?

A. The first condition of all is a vocation to the religious life.

Q. *62.* What is a vocation?

A. A vocation is a call from God to embrace a definite state of life. In this case, it is a call to embrace the religious life.

Q. *63.* How does one recognize a true vocation?

A. In the first place, one recognizes it by sensing the agreement of his inner desires and spiritual needs with the state to be embraced. He confirms this inner sentiment by means of good counsel from prudent persons, particularly from his confessor and spiritual director. Above all, he asks for and awaits illumination from God through prayer.

Q. *64.* Besides a vocation, what other conditions are required for valid admission into religion?

A. The following conditions are required by the Code for a person validly to be admitted into a religion upon his request:

1. That he be a Catholic (can. 538).

Excluded, then, are the nonbaptized, such as Jews, Mohammedans, infidels of any kind. Excluded also are persons baptized and educated in the Catholic faith, but who later have joined an heretical sect (can. 502, 1).

Protestants and heretics of whatever sect born in heresy but afterwards converted to Catholicism can be received into religion without any dispensation whatever (see the decision of the Pontifical Commission for the Interpretation of the Code, October 16, 1919).

2. That he be free of any lawful impediment (can. 538). The following, therefore, are excluded:

a. those who would enter religion under duress or under grave fear, or who are induced therein by deceit, or who are received by a superior who himself labors under grave fear, or is deceived, or is forced (can. 542, 1).

All persons, no matter how dignified their office, who have in any way forced a man or woman to enter religion or to make religious profession, solemn or simple, perpetual or temporary, are *ipso facto* under excommunication not reserved (can. 2352);

b. those who are still bound in matrimony (can. 542, 1).

Mention is no longer made in the Code of the possibility on the part of married persons of entering religion by mutual agreement. It therefore seems valid to conclude that once a true marriage has been contracted the parties fall under the diriment impediment which prevents their entrance into religion. This impediment, however, is purely from ecclesiastical law, wherefore the pope for grave reasons can dispense persons so involved.

No impediment remains for widowers or widows, nor for those persons whose marriage, in any way contracted, has been annulled (can. 542, 1).

c. those who are still professed in another religious institute or who have made a profession in any religious institute (can. 542, 1);

The phrase "made a profession" refers to those who, having completed their simple temporary vows or having been dispensed from them before their expiration have left religion.

"Who are still professed" refers to fugitives, apostates, and all those who, remaining in or out of the monastery, are still bound by vows taken in religious profession.

d. those who are in danger of being punished for a grave crime of which they stand accused, or for which it is foreseen that they could be indicted (can. 542, 1).

"A grave crime" means homicide, grand larceny, adultery, and the like, of which they already are accused or of which it is foreseen that they will be accused. A crime secretly committed is not meant here; the impediment refers only to a public crime which has already reached indictment or can easily reach indictment before a civil or ecclesiastical tribunal.

Q. 65. What else is required by the Code to make admission into religion not only valid but licit?
A. The following are demanded for licit admission:

1. That the candidate be motivated by a right intention (can. 538). He must have a true vocation and want to become a religious for no other purpose than to consecrate himself to the Lord in the practice of religious perfection.

2. That he be capable of observing the rules in religion. Excluded, therefore, are:

a. the infirm and those incapable from the start of practicing with regularity the austerities and the other observances of religion;

b. those afflicted with mental illnesses or so lacking in intelligence as to be incapable of understanding what is meant by religious perfection and the obligation to tend to it;

c. those who are so monstrous and deformed in body that they will expose the religious habit, when it is put on, to ridicule and insult;

d. those who show passionate tendencies or a proneness to other vices so inbred as seriously to put into doubt their reform, as, for example, when one is inclined to extreme irascibility or is pitifully weak in suppressing sensual passions.

3. That he be free from the following impediments:

a. *of debts.* He must have no debts which he cannot liquidate (can. 542, 2). This impediment lapses when either he himself or another for him settles with the creditors.

b. *of duties.* He must not have to answer for the administration of affairs, and must not be embroiled in affairs which can go into litigation to the embarrassment of the institute he wishes to enter (can. 542, 2). Whoever finds himself in these circumstances should first free himself from these involvements before asking to be admitted into religion.

c. *of filial obligations.* His parents or grandparents must not be in such need as absolutely to require his assistance. St. Thomas says on this point: "Whoever is still in the world and has parents in such a condition that without him they cannot properly provide for themselves, must not abandon them to enter religion, because he would trespass against the divine precept which obliges one to honor his father and his mother" (*Summa theol.,* II–II, q. 101, a. 4, ad 4m).

By parents, we mean, of course, one's own father and mother, and those who have exercised this office in his regard.

By grandparents, we mean the natural ones from the maternal as well as from the paternal side.

There is no mention of brothers or sisters, of nephews, nieces, cousins and the like, in the canon cited. Therefore, although in particular cases charity might oblige one to suspend or retard his entrance into religion to take care of a brother, a sister or other kinsman, the rule remains that there is no obligation to neglect one's vocation solely for the sake of taking care of one of these.

d. *of family obligations.* If the candidates are widowers or widows, they must no longer be needed for the support and education of their own children. St. Thomas (*ibid.,* IIa–IIae, q. 189, a. 6) states that it is not licit for one who has children to enter religion, neglecting the care one must have of them or without providing a good education for them. Further, we read in the Epistle to Timothy: "If any man have not care of his own and especially of those of his house, he hath denied the faith and is worse than an infidel" (I Tim., 5, 9).

e. *of rite*. He must not belong to an Oriental rite of the Catholic Church if it is a question of his wishing to enter a religious institute of the Latin rite. For a Catholic of the Oriental rite to enter an institute of the Latin rite the written permission of the Sacred Congregation for the Oriental Church is necessary (can. 542, 2).

f. *of irregularity*. If the person seeking admission into religion is also to be advanced to the priesthood, he must be free of all impediments to that order and from any irregularity (can. 542, 2).

Chapter 7

Postulancy

Q. 66. What is postulancy?
A. Postulancy is that period of time which intervenes between the acceptance of a person into religion and the beginning of the novitiate; in which period the candidate lives in the convent and follows the routine of the community under the vigilance of the superiors of the institute.

Q. 67. Is the postulancy always required?
A. In female religious institutes of perpetual vows the postulancy is always required of all candidates. In male religious institutes those who apply to become lay brothers or lay religious must make the postulancy (can. 539, 1).

In religious institutes wherein only temporary vows are taken the postulancy is never required by the common law of the Church. It might be required, however, by the constitutions of the various institutes.

Q. 68. How long must the postulancy last?
A. When the postulancy is demanded by the laws of the Church, as in the case of institutes in which perpetual vows are taken, it must last for at least six full months. It is within the power of the major superiors to extend it further, but never beyond another six months. When the postulancy is required

only by the constitutions, as in institutes of temporary vows, the constitutions must be followed in what they say about its duration (can. 539, 1 and 2).

Q. 69. Is it necessary that the six months of postulancy, besides being completed, must also be continuous or without interruption?
A. Probably not. When the Code demands continuity of time it expressly imposes it, as in the case of the novitiate. Therefore, absence from the monastery for some days, fifteen or twenty, does not seem to break the postulancy. The Code does not even demand that the days of absence be made up.

Q. 70. Where must the postulancy be made?
A. The postulancy must be made in the novitiate, or at least in another house of the institute wherein the regular discipline in harmony with the constitutions is in full force (can. 540, 1).

Q. 71. May the postulancy be made in several houses?
A. We believe so, as long as the houses verify the conditions laid down by the Code for the postulancy.

Q. 72. The postulancy completed is there an obligation to start the novitiate immediately, or can there be a delay?
A. Common practice is to start the novitiate immediately, but there does not seem to be any obligation. It is said in the Code that the candidates in a religion of perpetual vows, if they be women or destined for the lay brotherhood, must make a postulancy before the beginning of their novitiate, but it does not state that the novitiate should start immediately upon the expiration of the period of postulancy. Hence, if the candidate has completed the six months of required postulancy, or any further time under half a year demanded by a major superior, the starting of his novitiate, for any reasonable cause may be delayed, even notably, without requiring that the postulancy be repeated.

Q. 73. Does the shortening of the postulancy or dispensing with it entirely make invalid the novitiate and the profession?

A. It does not seem so. In view of the fact that the Code, when speaking of the obligation of the postulancy, does not mention any invalidating penalty, it would seem that its omission falls only under the category of the illicit.

Q. 74. May the postulancy begin before the age required for the novitiate?

A. It may begin at least six months before the completion of the fifteenth year. The Code does not expressly say so, but it does say that the novitiate may begin as soon as the fifteenth year is completed (can. 555, 1, 1). Evidently, then, the postulancy, which must precede the novitiate and last at least six months, can begin six months before the completion of the fifteenth year.

Q. 75. Who is to be in charge of the postulants?

A. A religious of exemplary life under whose vigilance the postulants are placed (can. 540, 1).

Q. 76. During the postulancy, is it required that a religious habit be worn?

A. By the law of the Church, no. However, it may be required by the constitutions. In this case, the Code prescribes that the dress of the postulants be different from the dress of the novices (can. 540, 2).

Q. 77. In cloistered monasteries, is it obligatory for the female postulants to observe enclosure?

A. Certainly (can. 541, 3). Therefore, in monasteries of nuns, the candidates, from the moment they are accepted as religious, may enter the cloister without need of special permission; but once they have entered, they may not leave it without special permission of the Holy See. Of course they may leave it if they intend to quit the institute.

Excepted from this provision are the extern sisters who make their postulancy in the house proper to extern sisters, that is, outside the cloister. These, however, must wear a modest dress or habit different from that of the novices (Sacred Congregation of Religious, July 16, 1931, Statutes, no. 22).

Q. 78. In a monastery of nuns, if a postulant leaves the cloister without due permission, does she incur excommunication?

A. No. The excommunication binds only the nuns who leave illicitly after their profession. Postulants, strictly speaking, are not nuns, much less professed nuns (can. 601, and 2342, 3). However, once the postulants have entered the cloister, they cannot leave and re-enter at pleasure.

Q. 79. Do the postulants enjoy the privileges, graces, and indulgences which the professed do?

A. It seems that they do not, on the strength of the decree of the Pontifical Commission with reference to the funerals of postulants. If these do not enjoy funeral privileges as religious do it would seem to indicate that they enjoy no other privileges of religious.

Q. 80. Have the postulants a right to suffrages like the professed?

A. No, unless the constitutions expressly declare the opposite. Suffrages are more than a grace or privilege: they are a right to the spiritual goods of an order or religious congregation in correlation with the burdens of the religious life. Postulants as yet have not contracted any burden, hence they have not even a relative right. It is different with the novices, for whom the law itself determines that they have a right to suffrages (see Q. 102).

Chapter 8

The Novitiate

Q. *81.* What is the novitiate?

A. The novitiate is that period of time given to a candidate for the religious life so that he can become acquainted beforehand with the rule of the institute and actually live it, and during which the institute itself, before admitting the candidate into actual membership, can assure itself concerning the disposition, habits, intelligence, and capacities of the aspirant (can. 565, and 571).

Q. *82.* What is the purpose of the novitiate?

A. The purpose of the novitiate in religious institutes is threefold:

1. that the novice may try out the austerities of the life, advance to a practical knowledge of the rule and routine, and thus find out for himself if he is capable of observing them faithfully;

2. that the religious institute may better acquaint itself with the qualifications of the candidate, lest unworthy ones be admitted;

3. that, for the mutual benefit of the candidate and the institute, the novice can habituate himself to the kind of life which he will have to lead.

Q. *83.* Where must the novitiate be made?
A. The novitiate must be made in that house assigned for this specific purpose (can. 555, 1, 3).

Q. *84.* Is that novitiate valid which is begun in one house and continued in another?
A. It is valid as long as both houses are novitiates of the same institute and the interruption has not exceeded thirty days. In this case, it is simply a change of locality, since the novitiate formally endures and continues to fulfill the purpose of proving the novice (can. 566, 4).

Q. *85.* What conditions are required by the Code for admittance into the novitiate?
A. The following are required by the Code for admittance into the novitiate:

1. All the conditions above enumerated for valid and licit acceptance in a religion are first to be satisfied (see Qq. 64, 65).

2. The candidate must have completed fifteen years of age (can. 432, 1; 555, 1, 1). This condition must be observed under penalty of invalidating the novitiate.

The reckoning of the years is to be made according to the norm of can. 34, 3, 3, namely, the hour of birth is not to be made the starting point, but the day of birth, a canonical year ending on that day's end. Thus, if one had been born at eleven o'clock on the morning of December 25, 1940, he completes his fifteenth year at the end of December 25, 1955. His novitiate cannot begin before midnight of December 25, 1955, but must start on December 26th or on any day thereafter.

3. He must have testimonial letters, that is, documents from competent ecclesiastical authorities attesting to certain facts necessary to qualify him for the religious life; for instance, that he was baptized and confirmed, that he is of good morals and is free of any matrimonial bond (can. 544, 2).

4. He must have the consent of those religious who, according to the norms of their own constitutions, have the right

to vote for or against the admission of new members (can. 543). If such a vote be required by the constitutions, it must be taken under penalty of invalidating the admission. It is enough, however, that he secure a majority vote assenting to his admission, a unanimous vote not being necessary.

5. If it is the question of a female seeking to become a nun, she must bring a dowry (can. 547, 1). If she is to become a sister, the question of bringing a dowry will depend on the particular constitutions (can. 547, 3).

When the dowry is prescribed in institutes of papal law, it cannot be dispensed with in whole or in part without an indult from the Holy See. In institutes of diocesan law it is sufficient to obtain the permission of the ordinary of the place to dispense with it (can. 547, 4).

6. A course of spiritual exercises of at least eight full days must precede the beginning of the novitiate (can. 541). Should the confessor judge it expedient, it is well to make beforehand a general confession of one's whole life (can. 541).

"Eight full days" will require that if the retreat is only for eight days, the first day and the last day must be spent entirely in spiritual exercises.

7. Each female candidate for the novitiate must be given a canonical examination (can. 552, 2).

Q. *86.* In what does this canonical examination consist, and by whom should it be made?
A. The canonical examination should be made by the bishop of the place or by a priest delegated by him. It consists principally in exploring the willingness of the postulant to embrace the religious life freely and conscientiously (can. 552, 2).

Q. *87.* When must this canonical examination take place?
A. At least thirty days before the investiture. The superioress has the strict obligation of letting the bishop know two months before the ceremony of reception so that he can make provision in time for the required examination (can. 552, 1).

Q. 88. Who can admit one to the novitiate?
A. The right of admitting one to the novitiate belongs to the major superiors by vote of the council and of the chapter, in the manner prescribed by their constitutions (can. 543).

Q. 89. When and how must the novitiate start?
A. The novitiate begins with the formal conferring of the religious habit, or in any other manner determined by the constitutions (can. 553).

It must be noted that in those religious institutes whose members fall into several distinct categories, for example, clerics and lay brothers or laymen, among men; choral religious and lay sisters, among women, the novitiate entered into for one category does not hold for another category (can. 558). If a transfer from one category to another is to be made, the novitiate must be started again for the new category, and even completely repeated if the transfer is made after profession.

Q. 90. What conditions are to be verified for the novitiate to start in regular manner?
A. For the novitiate to start in regular manner the Code requires the verification of the following conditions:

1. that the postulancy has been made in regular manner as it is prescribed either by the Code or by the constitutions (can. 539, 1; see also Q. 66 ff.);

2. that the investiture with the religious habit has been canonically made, as prescribed by the constitutions. Canon 557 reads: "The entire period of the novitiate is to be spent in the habit which the constitutions prescribe for novices, unless special circumstances of the place counsel otherwise." One special circumstance is a period of religious persecution.

3. the novice must be in residence in the house determined for the novitiate (can. 555, 1, 3). As we said above (Q. 83), the novitiate cannot be made in any house of the institute except

the one designated as the novitiate, and this under penalty of invalidating the novitiate.

Q. 91. Must a professed religious of either sex, who by permission of the Holy See passes from one religious institute to another, make a new novitiate in the habit of the religion he now desires to embrace?

A. The Sacred Congregation of Religious on May 14, 1923, replied in the affirmative.

Q. 92. How long must the novitiate last?

A. In every religious institute the novitiate must last at least one full and continuous year under penalty of making the profession null and void (can. 555, 1, 2).

The year is to be computed according to the calendar; hence if the novitiate began October 1st, it ends on October 1st of the following year, even if there be question of a leap year.

For the year to be integral it is necessary to compute from the end of the day on which the novitiate was started to the year following, regardless of the hour in which the novitiate started. Thus, if the novitiate began at eight in the morning of September 30th, the year of novitiate does not end at eight o'clock of the morning of September 30th of the following year, but at midnight of the 30th, so that the profession cannot be made until October 1st has begun (can. 555, 2).

Q. 93. May the novitiate last for more than a year?

A. It may last for more than a year, even for two years, if the constitutions prescribe it. However, if it is prescribed by the constitutions that the novitiate should last more than a year, time in excess of one year is not required under penalty of invalidating the profession, unless this is expressly stated in the constitutions (can. 555, 2).

Therefore, the Code does not forbid a religious institute to require constitutionally a novitiate of longer than a year.

However, that which is over and above a year's duration does not affect the validity of the profession, unless the same constitutions expressly say so.

Q. *94.* Can the novitiate be prolonged beyond the time determined by the Code or constitutions?
A. Yes, by action of the major superiors. If when the novitiate is finished as prescribed by the Code or constitutions, there remains any doubt as to the fitness of the subject, the major superiors can prolong the probation a bit further, but never more than six months (can. 571, 2).

Thus, if a year's novitiate has been prescribed, it can be extended to eighteen months; if a two-year novitiate has been started, it can be extended to thirty months in particular cases by action of the major superiors.

Q. *95.* In what way is the novitiate interrupted?
A. The novitiate can be interrupted in various ways, some of which so destroy the continuity of the novitiate as to bind the novice under penalty of invalidating his profession, in which case he will have to start it over again; while other interruptions oblige him merely to make up the days lost (can. 556).

Q. *96.* When must an interrupted novitiate begin over again?
A. In three cases:
1. If the novice, dismissed by the lawful superiors, has actually left the house of novitiate (can. 556, 1).

Thus, if the novice has been dismissed but has not as yet left the house, should the dismissal for any reason be revoked before he has left the house, the novitiate is not interrupted.

2. If the novice, without any permission of the superiors, leaves the novitiate with the intention not to return (can. 558, 1).

The intention not to return must be manifested externally by some overt act. The internal intention alone does not of itself interrupt the novitiate.

3. If, while having the intention of returning, he actually remains out of the house of novitiate for more than thirty days, whether they be consecutive or by interval, for whatever reason, and even if he had the full permission of his superiors for each absence (can. 556, 1).

"Whether they be consecutive or by interval" means that no matter if the thirty or more days follow each other without a break, or if the sum total of the days spent at various times outside the novitiate amounts to thirty days or more, the novitiate is broken and must be repeated.

"For whatever reason" includes even the most just of reasons, for example, a grave illness, a fire in the house, the death of a parent, the journeying from one novitiate to another (Commission on the Interpretation of the Code, July 13, 1930).

"Outside the house of novitiate" means the whole house, not just the novitiate portion. Although normally the novices should dwell in a separate part of the religious house, if, for any reason, one should dwell for a time outside the place of novitiate, as, for example, in the infirmary, he does not interrupt his novitiate, for he has not been outside the house of novitiate.

Q. 97. Is the novitiate interrupted if the novice remains for some days in a villa or country house of the institute for reasons of health or for any other motive?

A. Certainly, unless an Apostolic indult for it has been granted; for, while the villa or country house belongs to the convent and is destined for the use of the convent, it is not the convent, nor even a part of it, and it follows that it cannot be called a house of novitiate.

Q. 98. If the novitiate has been interrupted, when will it suffice merely to supply the days lost without need of starting it all over again?

A. If a novice, with the permission of his superiors, has remained outside the house of novitiate more than fifteen days, whether they be continuous or cumulative, it will suffice to supply the days lost by adding them to the time required for the novitiate. This is true also in the case wherein a novice has been forced, for example, by civil authorities or by parents, to remain outside the novitiate, although he continues under the obedience of his superiors. However, this does not apply if the days lost exceed thirty days (can. 556, 2).

"More than fifteen days" means that if the interruption by sum total does not exceed fifteen days, the making up of them is left to the discretion of the superiors who can demand it or not without prejudice to the validity of the profession (can. 556, 2).

"Exceed thirty days" means that if the total interruption amounts to more than thirty days the novitiate must begin over again, unless, of course, the Holy See grants a dispensation.

Q. 99. If a novice remains outside the house of novitiate for more than fifteen days, but less than thirty, is it enough for him to supply the actual days lost or only those over the fifteen?

A. He has to make up for all the days spent outside the house of novitiate, not alone those over the fifteen (can. 556, 2).

Q. 100. Does a novice who leaves the monastery at 10 o'clock in the morning on Monday and returns at 10 o'clock Tuesday evening interrupt his novitiate?

A. It seems that he does not, for the Code in speaking of interruption of the novitiate speaks of days and not of hours. Since, according to the Code, the day consists of twenty-four hours computed from midnight to midnight, in the present case we have thirty-six hours of absence, but not twenty-four hours of absence from one midnight to another, and therefore not an entire day in the canonical sense according to the norm of canon 32.

Q. *101.* What are the duties of novices who have not as yet made profession with respect to the life of the community in which they find themselves?

A. Novices have the obligation of observing the rule and of being subject to their proper superiors, not indeed by force of the vow of obedience, which as yet they have not taken, but by force of the virtue of obedience which they have tacitly promised by their very entrance into religion, and which renders them subject to their legitimate superiors as long as they remain therein; also by force of their vocation, inasmuch as having to make an experiment of it, they are obliged in conscience to do whatever may conspire to a successful outcome of the experiment. The observance of the rule and obedience to one's superiors are certainly among the bests ways of finding out one's own capacity for the life.

Q. *102.* Do novices enjoy even before their profession the privileges and spiritual graces of the religious institute?

A. They certainly do (can. 567, 1). From the moment of their investiture novices are accorded the favorable things in law, that is, things which result to their advantage as religious. They enjoy, therefore, all the graces and privileges granted to their religious institute. Wherefore:

1. They can gain all the indulgences which professed religious of the institute can gain.

2. If they should die before profession, they have a right to the same suffrages as the professed religious.

These prescriptions of the Code with reference to the suffrages hold even if the constitutions approved before the Code may expressly deny such (can. 439; see also the reply of the Pontifical Commission for the Interpretation of the Code under date of October 16, 1919). Should this grant prove too onerous, religious institutes have the right to submit new constitutions for approval before the Sacred Congregation of Religious fixing a new list of suffrages, which, however, must always be the same for novices as for the professed, whether of simple or solemn vows, temporary or perpetual (The Pontifical Commission as cited above, October 19, 1919).

Q. 103. Are novices in a monastery of nuns bound to observe the cloister?

A. Certainly. If the Code imposes such for the postulants (can. 540), with even greater reason must we say that novices are held to it.

Similarly, if the law of the cloister exists in a house of sisters, its novices must observe it according to the tenor of the constitutions.

Q. 104. Is the novice free to leave the religious house if it no longer pleases him or her to remain?

A. The novice is absolutely free to leave (can. 571, 1). As was said above, the novitiate is established precisely for the purpose of having the novice make a trial of the rule and the routine of life before taking vows.

"Absolutely free" we say, provided that the novice in leaving does not violate any right of the religion, or that the religion cannot advance any reason for restraining him. He who has felt a true vocation must in conscience do everything possible on his part to realize the vocation.

Q. 105. May the superiors of an institute dismiss a novice when they wish to do so?

A. They may, most surely, as long as there is a justifying reason (can. 571, 1).

A good reason is always required, otherwise the superiors would sin against charity by unjustly hindering the novice from realizing his vocation and by depriving the religion of a useful member sent by God for the good of the religion.

Q. 106. Who is in charge of the training of the novices?

A. The master of novices for men, the mistress of novices for women (can. 550, 1).

Q. *107.* Of what age of life and years of profession, according to the Code, must the master or mistress of novices be?

A. At least thirty-five years of age, and ten of profession, computed from the first profession when there is a first (can. 550, 1). It is sufficient that the thirty-fifth year of life has been started, but the ten years of profession must be complete (can. 34, 3).

Q. *108.* Of what age of life and years of profession must the submaster or submistress be?

A. These must be at least thirty years of age and five of profession, computed from the first profession (can. 599, 2). Here again it is sufficient that the thirtieth year has been started, while the five years of profession must be complete (can. 34, 3).

~~~~~~~~~~~~~~~~~~

Chapter 9

The Vows

~~~~~~~~~~~~~~~~~~

Q. *109.* What is a vow?
A. A vow is a promise made to God of a possible and better thing (can. 1307, 1).

Q. *110.* What is meant by the word "promise"?
A. It does not mean a simple proposal to do or not to do a certain thing, reserving to oneself full freedom to do even the opposite if it should so please him; but it does mean a deliberate will to do or not to do that certain thing with the intention of binding oneself in conscience to it.

There is no need, then, of confusing a vow with those promises to do or not to do a certain thing without the intention of binding oneself strictly in conscience, as, for example, out of devotion daily to recite the Rosary or to perform other pious actions. These are indeed good proposals in better things, but since in their very formulation they lack the intention of contracting an obligation in conscience, they are not considered as vows, and, indeed, are not vows.

Q. *111.* Why is it said that the promise is made to God?
A. Because, although the vows can be made in honor of and

invoking the aid of the Blessed Virgin and the saints, to be truly vows they must be made directly and principally always to God, with whom one desires to contract the obligation for their observance in true conscience.

Q. *112.* Why is it said, "of a possible thing"?
A. Because in truth one cannot have a serious will to do a thing which, everything considered, is morally or physically impossible. A vow to eat iron instead of bread would not be valid, for that is a thing physically impossible. Likewise, a vow to recite continuously, without any interruption, the Ave Maria, is morally impossible of fulfillment.

Q. *113.* Why is it said, "of a better thing"?
A. Because a vow is an act of perfection, or at least a means of tending to perfection. This meaning of a vow is not verified if the thing vowed is not better than its opposite.

We know from the Gospel that it is the will of God that we tend to perfection. "Be ye perfect as your heavenly Father is perfect." We know, too, that a vow, to have any worth, must be accepted by God, which means, therefore, that it must be pleasing and acceptable to Him. How can God accept a promise that would bind us to lesser perfection? God's will for us to be perfect demands that we keep tending to the more perfect. For example, we know from the Gospel that it is more perfect to divest ourselves, out of love for poverty, even of those goods which we can lawfully possess, or which we could keep accumulating through honest methods. Again, according to the Gospel, we know that it is more perfect to fast out of love for Christian mortification, than to enjoy a sumptuous banquet. Without doubt, therefore, we can make a vow of poverty out of a desire to divest ourselves of our lawful material possessions; we can make a vow to fast on Fridays, or to abstain from milk products. It would be most incongruous, on the other hand, to make a vow to enrich ourselves or to feast sumptuously every day.

Q. 114. What is the proper effect of each vow?

A. The proper effect of each vow, whatever it be, is that its fulfillment becomes an act of the virtue of religion; of that virtue, namely, by which we render to God the honor and worship due to Him. Therefore, it is the most excellent of all the moral virtues, while the breaking of the vow becomes a sin against the virtue of religion, and is therefore a sacrilege (can. 1307, 1).

Q. 115. What are the "better" acts which we can promise by vows?

A. We can reduce them to three classes:
1. the acts already obligatory for Christian living;
2. the acts which are of counsel;
3. the acts which are morally indifferent. Sinful acts can never be made objects of a vow.

The acts already obligatory. In this case, the vow adds to the obligation already existing a second obligation, that of the vow itself, the new obligation arising out of the fact that a vow is an act of the virtue of religion and consequently, it brings double guilt when the vow is not fulfilled, but it carries double merit when it is fulfilled. For example, he who takes the vow of chastity obliges himself doubly to chaste living, first, by virtue of the sixth and ninth commandments, and again by virtue of the second commandment. Thus in one vow he is practicing two virtues, the virtue of chastity and that of religion. This is why the observance of chastity by vow becomes "a better thing."

The acts of counsel. A good example of this is not to contract matrimony though free to do so. Even in this case the vow adds a new dignity to something already good in itself; indeed, it brings it to greater excellence. We know from the Gospel that to abstain from marriage, that is, to practice perfect chastity out of love for our Savior is already an evangelical counsel, an act for the better (Matt. 19, 12). Moreover, to oblige oneself by vow to do so makes the act still more perfect.

The acts morally indifferent. These, in themselves, are neither good nor bad, as, for example, to walk. However, they acquire a morality, becoming good or bad through the intention by which they are performed. Thus, to walk for reasons of health makes walking a good act. Now besides the intention there is another means of rendering these indifferent acts good and meritorious, namely, by doing them or avoiding them by vow, since through the vow they acquire a new goodness, which is the goodness and the merit of the virtue of religion. For example, it is lawful to vow not to take a walk in the morning so as to have more time to study, because such an act by reason of the intention is better than its opposite. By virtue of the vow, therefore, there is added to the act a new goodness, namely the goodness and the merit of the virtue of religion.

Q. 116. What is the gravity of the obligation contracted by the vow?

A. If the thing promised by vow is in itself grave, it is understood, unless the contrary has been mentioned, to oblige gravely, that is, under pain of mortal sin. However, since this obligation contracted by the vow is one which is freely imposed on oneself, there is no reason why, even if the matter promised by the vow be in itself grave, it could not be made obligatory under pain of venial sin if the one making the vow expressly intended so to bind himself. Similarly, the one who vows is always free to determine the other circumstances, such as time, place, and so on, in which the vow is to be fulfilled.

Q. 117. Is this equally true concerning the vows taken in religious profession?

A. No, because it is already fixed by law that the members of a religious institute must all make their profession in the same manner, all conforming to the same rule and contracting the same obligations. One is free to make profession or not; but if he makes profession, he must make it by contractual vows which impose obligations conformable to the laws of the

Church and to the constitutions of the institute in which he
makes profession.

Q. 118. Why must religious vows, besides being conformable
to the laws of the Church, be conformable also to the constitutions of a particular religious institute?

A. For the reason which follows: The three religious vows
of poverty, chastity, and obedience are in themselves essential
elements of the religious state regardless of the institute one
enters. Indeed, they are so essential that if all three vows be
not taken in profession, we can have only something similar
to, but not truly, the religious state (see Q. 26, note 2). The
religious vows, however, differ with reference to the manner
of observing them. For example, the vow of poverty is observed
with more or less rigor, varying with the spirit of each order
or religious institute. Hence, it is necessary to express in the
formula of profession that the vows are taken "in conformity
with the rule and constitutions" of one's own institute.

Q. 119. What difference in matter is there with respect to
poverty, chastity, and obedience between the vow and the
virtue?

A. There are several differences. First of all, there is an intrinsic difference, inasmuch as the direct object of the vow is
negative, a privation imposed on oneself by him who vows, as
when he deprives himself of temporal goods; while, in contrast,
the direct object of the virtue is positive, that is, to regulate, as
in the case of poverty, the affections for things of earth and
the good use of earthly goods. By consequence, the virtue under
this aspect is something more perfect than the vow for it is
precisely for the purpose of acquiring more securely, more
easily and more fully this very virtue that the religious is inspired to take the vow.

Further, the object of the virtue, at least in the two vows
of poverty and obedience, is more extensive than that of the
vow, wherefore it is possible to sin against the virtue without

sinning against the vow, but not vice versa. For example, a religious who does not obey the lawful civil authority sins against the virtue of obedience, but does not sin against the vow, not having contracted, when he made profession, to include this obedience as well, for he owes obedience by vow only to his lawful religious superiors.

The vow, however, has this excellence, that to the goodness of the moral virtue to which the vow is referred, it adds the goodness and merit of the virtue of religion. Thus it transforms and elevates the proper acts of the virtue to which the vow refers, whether of poverty, chastity, or obedience, to acts of divine worship before God, that is, to acts of another virtue, that of religion, specifically different from the first. By consequence, the vow acquires a new specific goodness, a double merit. Under this aspect the vow becomes a means of great perfection.

Q. 120. Why are the religious vows called evangelical counsels?

A. Because, while not being obligatory, they are suggested in the Gospels as a good thing, indeed, a higher thing. They were counselled by our Lord Jesus Christ as efficacious means of tending to perfection, in contrast to the precepts of the Gospel which are indicated in the sacred pages as the indispensable means for the winning of eternal life.

Q. 121. Besides the three vows of poverty, chastity, and obedience, may other vows be taken in the religious profession?

A. Certainly. Members of some orders and religious congregations take, for example, the vow to go to the missions, the vow to serve in hospitals, to abstain from meat perpetually, and so on. It remains true, however, that the first three vows are essential in every form of religious life, so much so that without them the Church disclaims the existence of a truly religious state. These other vows are added only by virtue of the constitutions.

Chapter *10*

~~~~~~

The Various Kinds of Vows

~~~~~~

Q. *122.* Are all vows of the same kind?

A. No, they are divided into several kinds:

1. by reason of their duration, vows may be either temporary or perpetual;

2. by reason of the manner in which they are taken, vows may be either public or private;

3. by reason of their effects, vows may be either simple or solemn;

4. by reason of their dispensability, vows are either reserved or not reserved.

Q. *123.* What are temporary and what are perpetual vows?

A. Temporary vows are those which are taken for a determined period of time, for example, one year, three years, and the like.

Perpetual vows are those taken without limitation of time, namely, with the intention of keeping them for the rest of one's life.

Q. *124.* When are vows said to be public and when are they private?

A. Vows are said to be public when they are accepted by the lawful superior in the name of the Church (can. 1308, 1).

Vows are private, or of devotion, when they lack this official acceptance on the part of the Church.

Each of the faithful, if it so pleases him, can oblige himself before God to do something more in his Christian life than is absolutely required. He can, out of his particular devotion and fervor of spirit, make vows. However, the vows are considered private if the authority of the Church is not called upon to confirm them. In order that vows be considered public, the Church empowers religious superiors to accept them, in her name, in the form of a quasi-contract (see Q. 235).

Q. 125. Are the vows of religion made in a religious institute considered private or public?

A. Religious vows, to be truly those of religious, must always be public. Indeed, they are religious vows precisely because they are public, that is, accepted by the Church (can. 488, 1).

Q. 126. When are vows said to be reserved or not reserved?

A. Vows are not reserved when they can be dispensed by some ecclesiastical superior or by some confessor without need of referring the case to the Holy See.

Vows are said to be reserved when the Holy See reserves unto itself alone the power of dispensing from them (can. 1308, 3).

The only person who, in God's name, or as interpreter of God's will, can dispense from the obligation contracted by vow made to God is the Supreme Pontiff, the Vicar of Jesus Christ on earth. Sometimes the Holy Father reserves the dispensation to himself; sometimes for certain vows he permits a dispensation to be granted in his name either by the bishops, by some confessors, or by other ecclesiastical superiors. In the first case, the vows are said to be reserved; in the second case, not reserved.

Q. 127. Are religious vows reserved or not?

A. Religious vows, whether they be simple or solemn, if

validly pronounced in a religious institute of papal law are always reserved. If the institute is of diocesan law only, they are not reserved by the Holy See; wherefore the bishop can dispense from them (can. 638, 640).

Q. *128.* When are vows solemn and when are they simple?
A. Vows are solemn when the Church recognizes them as solemn (can. 1308, 1).

Vows are simple when the Church does not recognize them as solemn.

The acceptance, that is, the recognition on the part of the Church by declaring that a vow taken under this or that circumstance is truly solemn, is the indispensable condition whereby a vow becomes solemn and is the distinctive characteristic of a simple and a solemn vow.

Simple and solemn vows differ also by reason of their effects which juridically follow, as will be discussed later (Qq. 155, 156, 189, 190, 208, 209).

Theologians and canonists are not in agreement as to whether there is further need of consolidating the difference between simple and solemn vows through an intrinsic element.

They who say there is an intrinsic distinction find it in this: The simple vow promises God only the surrender of the right to use the thing sacrificed by vow, for example, the right to use one's property. The solemn vow, on the other hand, entails the surrender of the material good itself and of its use, that is, it deprives one of the right to use his riches and even divests him of proprietary rights to the same. In this manner the surrender to God of one's temporal goods is complete and unconditional. The followers of St. Thomas adhere to this opinion, which seems better grounded and which truly imparts to the solemn vow a special solemnity, while it gives to the profession of it the true meaning of sacrifice, or, better still, of a holocaust offered to God.

Q. *129.* What kinds of vows are taken in religious orders properly so called?

A. In religious orders solemn vows are taken (can. 488, 2). They are not taken immediately, but after a period of temporary vows, as we will explain in Q. 264.

Q. 130. In so-called religious congregations what kinds of vows are taken?
A. In religious congregations the vows are always simple, even if they are perpetual (can. 488, 2).

Q. 131. Would it not be better to take only solemn vows?
A. Solemn vows, considered in themselves, are certainly more perfect and more efficacious means of perfection than simple vows, as we have said above. However, that which is in itself the more perfect is not always the more useful in practice. For this reason, the Church, for the attainment of the special end which some institutes have fixed for themselves, and also for the sake of prudence, has preferred and still prefers, particularly in new foundations of the active life, that the vows be simple and not solemn. The Church also demands today that even in those institutes wherein solemn vows are taken a certain period of simple vows should precede (can. 253).

Q. 132. What age is required for the pronouncing of religious vows?
A. For simple temporary vows the age of sixteen completed years is required for men and women. For solemn vows and simple perpetual vows the age of twenty-one completed years is required. All this is under penalty of invalidating the vows.

Q. 133. Do private vows taken before religious profession hold after profession?
A. Private vows taken before religious profession in any religious institute remain suspended as long as the person bound by such vows continues in religion (can. 1315).

"Remain suspended" means that the vows are neither dispensed with nor annulled, but the obligation to observe them ceases for the total period of one's membership in religion.

On that day, however, when a person who has taken private vows before his profession ceases to be a religious for any reason, such as the expiration, with nonrenewal, of the time of temporal profession, a dispensation, a dismissal, the vows taken before the profession acquire their previous binding force.

Q. 134. Would a vow hold if a religious were, out of devotion, to make a vow after profession?
A. Vows privately taken after one's religious profession without the permission of the superiors, if they be in no way burdensome on the religious, that is, if they are in no way incompatible with the obligations of the religious state already embraced, are of themselves valid, and therefore bind the religious to their observance. But if the superiors find such vows to be onerous to the religious life, they can declare that such vows made without their permission are null and void, and, therefore, can terminate them.

For a religious bound by solemn vows such private vows are of themselves invalid; for a religious bound by simple vows, they can be cancelled (can. 501, 1; 1312, 1).

Profession in religion ought not and cannot in itself impede the doing of more or better things than those implied by the strict observance of the religious life. Hence, if a religious, besides the obligation of the three vows of poverty, chastity, and obedience, makes a vow, for example, to be always humble, there is no reason why the religious profession should impede the exercise under vow of this beautiful virtue, which if faithfully observed in practice, is not only a great help towards perfection, but is also a great advantage for the observance of all the other points of the rule.

It is evident that religious, obliged as they are to the observance of the rule in dependence on their legitimate superiors, cannot contract obligations which might distract them from these prime duties. Superiors are not obliged to honor these new obligations even if the subject tells him he has already made the promise of them. This certainly holds for religious bound by solemn vows, for these, under pain of nullity, are incapable of contracting any onerous obligations without the permission of their superiors (can. 579). It is otherwise with religious of simple vows. Here, however, the superiors, in virtue of the dominative power they have over their subjects, can cancel any vow made after profession if the obligation of the private vow is of a nature to jeopardize the fulfillment of the prime duties contracted by the profession (can. 1312, 2; see also Q. 212).

It is understood, of course, that superiors, to be on the side of law, cannot act capriciously. They must have the intention of safeguarding the welfare of their subjects and of the community which they rule. Accordingly, although a just reason is not demanded for the validity of the cancellation, it is required so that the cancellation be licit (can. 1312, 1).

Q. *135.* Can vows that are private or out of devotion be annulled?

A. Yes, they can be annulled by the pope. In the cases contemplated by the Code, a dispensation from them can be given also by the ordinary and by anyone to whom has been conceded the delegation for the dispensation in singular cases (can. 1313).

Q. *136.* Can public religious vows be annulled?

A. Even these can be dispensed when there is a grave reason, but with this distinction: If they have been validly pronounced in an institute of papal law, they can be dispensed only by the pope; if they have been pronounced in an institute of diocesan law, then the ordinary of the place can dispense from them (can. 638, 640).

Q. *137.* The dispensation having been obtained, must it for validity be accepted by the religious for whom it has been requested?

A. Yes, except in particular cases, where the Sacred Congregation rules to the contrary (Sacred Congregation of Religious, August 11, 1922).

Q. 138. When do the temporary vows expire?
A. They expire at the end of *one year* according to canon 34, that is, at midnight of the anniversary day on which they had been taken.

Temporary vows for religious also expire at the moment of dismissal from an order or religious congregation (can. 648).

Q. 139. Is a vow temporary or perpetual when a religious, while making profession of temporary vows, intends to consecrate himself to God by a *perpetual* vow of chastity?
A. The vow of chastity, pronounced in a profession juridically temporary, is recognized as only temporary by the Church; but since there has been an expressed and determined intention on the part of the votary to consecrate himself perpetually to God in chastity, it obliges him personally, in conscience, as a perpetual vow of chastity. Wherefore, in the forum of conscience, with reference even to the dispensation which may later be required, the person's confessor shall so regard it. It cannot be presumed that the Church, with all her prudent prescriptions concerning temporary vows, intends to forbid explicitly, at least as a private vow, the resolve to consecrate oneself perpetually to God in chastity from the first day of his profession. At all events, as a religious vow it is legally valid only for the period for which the profession was made. The superiors of the religious are not obliged to take into account any private intention on the part of the one professing to bind himself perpetually.

~~~~~~~~~~~~~~~~~~~~~~~~~~~~~~~~~~~~

Chapter 11

The Vow of Poverty

~~~~~~~~~~~~~~~~~~~~~~~~~~~~~~~~~~~~

Q. 141. In what does the vow of poverty consist?
A. The vow of poverty consists in the renunciation, in the spirit of the Gospel, of dominion, or at least of the use and fruits of all the earthly goods one possesses.

Q. 142. What is meant by dominion?
A. We mean the right to possess as one's private property any worldly goods. It is of two kinds: radical dominion and useful dominion.

Q. 143. What is meant by radical dominion?
A. We mean the actual possession of a thing as one's own by him who has the dominion of it, without reference to its use or fruits.

Q. 144. What is meant by useful dominion?
A. We mean the power to dispose of a thing as to its use or its fruits, even if one does not have radical dominion over it.

Q. 145. What difference is there between use and fruits or
  yield?
A. Use is the power to dispose of a thing as to the usefulness

which one can derive from it, for example, the right to use a well for the drawing of water, even if the well belongs to another. Having the "fruits or yield" of a thing (in law commonly called usufruct) means the right to use not the thing itself, but the fruit it can yield; for example, the right to enjoy for ten years the harvest of grapes from a vineyard, though it is another man's property.

Q. 146. How many degrees are there in the vow of poverty?
A. This vow has four degrees:

1. the renunciation of superfluous things;

2. the renunciation of the free and independent use of necessary things;

3. the renunciation even of the dominion over goods, whether superfluous or necessary, which one possesses; and the renunciation of the right to acquire for oneself other goods;

4. the renunciation, finally, of the very right to possess or acquire any temporal goods, either individually or as a community.

Q. 147. What degree of poverty is absolutely necessary for the religious state?
A. For the essence of the religious state the second degree of poverty suffices as a minimum requirement. As regards perfection, without a doubt the higher the degree of poverty, the higher, objectively speaking, will be the vow.

Q. 148. What and how many are the degrees of perfection in the practice of poverty after taking the vow?
A. They are three:

1. being content with the use of things which are really necessary, and thereby excluding every superfluity;

2. the desire and preference for what is inferior and poorer among the goods of the community, for example, coarser garments, a homelier cell, etc. This is the first step towards the perfection of the virtue of poverty.

3. Convention permitting, giving up even that which is necessary, rejoicing in it if the Lord allows the religious to join
Him in one manner or another in His extreme poverty. This
is the degree most perfect in the practice of this virtue.

Q. 149. Is the vow of poverty necessary for the religious state?
A. It is necessary, because it conforms to the counsel given
by our Lord Jesus Christ to the young man who asked Him
what he should do to become perfect. "Go," said Jesus, "sell
what thou hast; give it to the poor, and come, follow Me"
(Matt. 19, 21; see also can. 487).

Q. 150. What objects does the vow of poverty take into consideration?
A. The vow of poverty considers as objects temporal things,
or, the things called temporal goods, such as money, credit, real
estate, a business, furniture, clothing, etc.

Q. 151. Do spiritual goods, such as honor and reputation,
come under the vow of poverty?
A. Absolutely speaking, no, because they are not things estimable in price or in the field of economics with market evaluation. Wherefore, religious retain, even after their profession,
the right to their good name, to their reputation, etc. This
does not mean, however, that through desire for greater perfection, when prudence and charity permit, a religious cannot
renounce in particular cases one or the other of these goods.
He is capable of and will advance more easily to perfection.

Q. 152. Do one's manuscripts, especially those prepared after
taking his vows, fall under the vow of poverty?
A. A doubt on this question was presented to the Sacred
Congregation of Religious, which under date of July 13, 1913
replied that manuscripts are included in the vow of poverty;
and justly so, because although personal or nonpersonal manuscripts are a direct product of one's intelligence, they are never-

theless temporal things estimable in price. What is said of manuscripts applies even more to rare books, copies of classical works, and so on.

Quite reasonable is the modern custom in religious institutes whereby religious, without having to ask any further permission of their superiors, keep and bring with them their own manuscripts when they go from one house to another in the same way that they bring their pious books, reference books, and so on.

Q. 153. Who is the owner of paintings, sculptures, and of any other art or craft work executed by a religious?
A. Paintings and sculptures are certainly works worth a price. In canon 580, 2, it is stated that whatever thing has a price, though produced or acquired by a religious through his industry, belongs to the community. Therefore, paintings, sculptures, and other art or craft works belong to the community and fall under the vow of poverty.

Q. 154. What are the effects of the vow of poverty?
A. They are varied, according as the vow is simple or solemn.

Q. 155. What are the effects of a simple vow of poverty?
A. The simple vow of poverty, whether temporary or perpetual, demands:

1. The renunciation of the lawful use and fruits of all of one's temporal goods, while keeping the radical dominion of these goods (can. 580, 1). This is to be done before the making of profession, as we shall see in Q. 256.

Consequently, after a religious makes profession and is bound by this vow he cannot licitly use his goods or dispose of their fruits for himself or for others without the permission of his superiors.

He can, however, retain the radical possession of the goods he owned before his profession and acquire new ones (can. 580, 1).

2. It demands also the renouncing of the administration of goods possessed, so that a religious bound by the vow of poverty cannot make contracts, or in any other way dispose of, or retain the administration of his goods without the permission of his superiors. Before profession the novice must cede to his superiors the administration of all his property (can. 569, 1).

Q. 156. What are the effects of the solemn vow of poverty?
A. The solemn vow of poverty demands:

1. The surrender or renunciation both of the useful and of the radical dominion over goods possessed (can. 580, 1). Qq. 141 and 142 have given the meaning of useful and radical dominion.

2. The legal incapacity or inability of the one making the vow to acquire other goods from whatever source, and not only proprietary rights over them, but even their use and usufruct (can. 562).

"The one making the vow" means the particular religious but not his institute. The solemn vow of poverty does not mean the incapacity of the community of which one is a member to acquire and possess property. With only a few exceptions, as in the case of orders strictly mendicant (see Q. 30 above), there is verified a proverb among religious of solemn vows, namely: "Whatever the monk acquires, the monastery acquires," that is, all that comes to the religious of solemn vows belongs to the monastery (can. 582).

3. The legal inability, without the permission of the superior, to make a will, to contract obligations, to stipulate agreements, etc., respecting the use, fruits, or proprietary rights of any temporal good (can. 581, 582).

Q. 157. In how many ways can the vow of poverty be violated?
A. Whether the vow be simple or solemn, it can be violated in three ways:

1. offending against the vow alone, that is, offending against the virtue of religion;

2. offending against both the virtue of religion and the virtue of poverty;

3. offending against three virtues, namely, religion, poverty, and justice.

Q. 158. When does a religious violate only his vow?
A. The religious offends against his vow only when, without the permission of his superiors, he accepts from outsiders temporal goods, keeps them, uses them, and liberally disposes of them in favor of others; similarly, if he administers or alienates the goods which he holds in radical dominion. In all these cases the religious goes counter to the promises he made to God concerning his rights, and he therefore acts illicitly, violating, however, only the virtue of religion.

Q. 159. When does the religious, failing in his vow, sin both against the vow and the virtue of justice?
A. The religious sins against both his vow and the virtue of justice when he appropriates the goods of another or even of his own institute without any permission of his superiors; or when he culpably destroys or dissipates these goods, bringing loss to his community. Hence, in these cases not only does he violate the promises made to God, but also the rights of others, and consequently he sins against justice.

Q. 160. When does a religious, failing in his vow, sin against all three of the virtues, namely, of religion, poverty, and justice?
A. When, with the unlawful appropriation or alienation of goods not his own, or even if they belong to his community, he adds an inordinate attachment and affection for these goods.

Q. 161. Can a religious fail in the virtue of poverty without failing in the vow?

A.   Yes, in two ways: first, through a misdirected affection and attachment for the things that are legitimately given for his use, and secondly, by the use of superfluous things, even if they are kept with the permission of the superiors.

Q.   162. Is not the retention by a religious of superfluous or ardently sought things against his vow?
A.   If he does it with due permission it is rather against the virtue than against the vow. It is always customary to avoid such retentions since one has the obligation to tend to perfection.

Q.   163. Does violation of the vow of poverty admit of smallness of matter? In other words, in order to commit a grave sin against the vow of poverty is there required a determined quantity?
A.   Certainly. Whether we are talking about the vow alone, or of those things which harm also the virtue of poverty, or of justice, the abuse of things not one's own or even one's own, always demands a minimum of matter for it to become a mortal sin.

Q.   164. What constitutes a mortal sin against the vow of poverty for a religious?
A.   Not all agree on the requisites necessary to constitute a mortal sin. Generally it is held that for a religious to commit a mortal sin against the vow of poverty there is needed the same amount of matter that is required of a member of a family with reference to goods taken away from the family. Thus the spending of a dollar by a religious without permission is certainly a sin, but not a grave one, as it would not be in the case of a member of a family. The spending, however, of a hundred dollars without permission is certainly materially sufficient for a grave sin on the part of a religious as it is for the member of a family.

Q. 165. Is it against the vow of poverty to receive gifts and offerings to give to the poor if these gifts and offerings are received and distributed without the permission of the superiors?

A. If any gift or offering is given by the donor with the definite and expressed intention of giving it for charity or alms to specified poor persons, the receiving and distributing of such gifts are not against the vow. In this instance the religious does not perform any proprietary act, but is simply an agent of the will of another. It is the donor who dispenses the gifts as he wills, using the religious merely as an aid in the giving.

If, however, the gift and offering are given to the religious to pass on to the poor without any expressed determination on the part of the donor, in this case it seems that the religious can neither take, much less keep, the gift and offering without at least the tacit permission of the superior. This is true even if the religious actually uses these gifts and offerings in alms for the poor. The selection of the poor to be helped and the determining of the amount of the alms to be distributed are aspects of acts of proprietorship, which it seems cannot be performed lawfully by religious without permission of the superiors.

Q. 166. May a religious give alms of the goods of the community without the permission of the superior?

A. He may not. Although it is an excellent thing to help the poor, the religious must have authorization by the superior. Otherwise, he acts as a proprietor, and, consequently, fails in the vow. It is understood that even a mere tacit or presumed permission will suffice, but some acquiescence on the part of the superior is absolutely necessary (see Q. 173).

Q. 167. How many kinds of permissions are there?

A. There are four kinds of permissions, namely, the expressed, the tacit, the implicit, and the presumed.

Q. 168. When is the permission expressed?
A. When the superior expresses, that is, formally manifests his will to permit or refuse a certain thing.

Q. 169. When is a permission said to be tacit?
A. The permission is called tacit when the superior consents by his very silence. He understands that for the performance of such and such a thing his permission is needed; he knows and sees that the thing is being done, nevertheless he makes no objection though he can do so. This conscious silence on the part of superiors is equivalent to tacit consent. Hence the adage, "silence is consent."

Q. 170. When is the permission said to be implicit?
A. It is called implicit when it is included in another permission expressly given, for example, if the superior gives one permission to go from Washington to New York, it is understood that implicitly he is giving permission for the necessary expenses of the journey.

Q. 171. When is the permission said to be presumed?
A. A presumed permission is that which in point of fact was not expressly given, nor tacitly nor implicitly given, but which it is reasonably presumed would be given were the superior to know the circumstances in which the religious finds himself (see Q. 174).

Q. 172. To act licitly in the matter of poverty does the having of any one of these permissions suffice?
A. Yes, the having of any one of these permissions will suffice, because in any case the permission of the superior in some way is had. However, one has to be very careful not to deceive himself in the matter of a tacit or presumed permission. It is always better to follow ordinary procedure which is to seek to act with the expressed, or at least with the clearly implied permission of the superior.

Q. 173. What is required so that a religious can lawfully act with tacit permission?

A. It is required that such a permission actually be there, that is, that the superior truly knows the case, tacitly agrees and does not command the opposite. For example, if a religious is accustomed to collect medals, images, and the like, to distribute them to children, to the sick, and so on, and the superior knows that he is actually doing so and yet does not forbid it, it can be said that he tacitly consents to it.

Q. 174. When can permission be presumed?

A. Permission can be presumed when it is a question of urgency and cannot be brought to the superior's attention, wherefore by reasonable interpretation of his mind it is presumed that he would not only grant the permission for it if he were asked, but would even be pleased by the use of the presumed permission in like circumstances. However, if there is anything in the process which remains within the competence of the superior to approve or not, he must be informed as to what was done at the first opportunity. For example, if a religious is given $100 for traveling expenses, and while traveling the opportunity presents itself of purchasing a book he badly needs at a most reasonable price, he may make the purchase, using part of the traveling money, but he must report it later to the superior.

Q. 175. Why is the performance of acts of proprietorship with permission not against the vow?

A. Because in that case the religious does not act as the master or possessor of the thing; he merely acts as an agent and simple executor of the will of the superior.

Q. 176. In what manner are the goods assigned for one's use to be kept so as to observe the vow of poverty?

A. Goods assigned for one's use are not to be kept as one's

own. Hence, he who conceals them in any way so as to remove
them from the free disposition of the superior, or is not sin-
cerely disposed to give them up at the pleasure of the superior
even without hope of regaining them, does not keep them
properly.

Q. *177.* What diligence must the religious exercise over the
things granted for his use?
A. He must exercise that diligence which a good and faithful
steward of another's goods customarily applies in good conscience. Wherefore, he must take every precaution that they be
not lost or badly consumed through his fault; neither may he
use them in quantity excessive of real need; nor should he be
negligent in their safe keeping.

Q. *178.* Does the religious who shows no care of the things
given for his use sin against the vow?
A. Certainly, if the negligence is culpable. He has a definite
obligation of guarding the things given for his use, as is expected of any faithful custodian of goods not his own. Things
are given to him with that understanding and under such
obligations. If he does not observe them, he fails in the pledges
undertaken in the matter of poverty and consequently he
offends against the vow.

Q. *179.* With reference to poverty, what is implied by the
term "common life"?
A. Common life among religious consists in this, that "all the
temporal goods are placed and administered in common, each
religious receiving from the common store whatever is needed
in food and clothing (can. 594, 1).

Q. *180.* Is the common life obligatory in religion?
A. The first article of canon 594 reads: "In every religious
institute all must carefully observe the common life."

Q. 181. What canonical penalties does a religious incur who violates the vow of poverty?

A. Before the Code there had been fixed in the common law various penalties against those who might violate the vow of poverty made in religious institutes, among which most notable were those of privation of a church burial and loss of active and passive voice for two years. However, the Code no longer mentions these penalties. They can, of course, be inserted in the constitutions of each institute, if they so wish, but they no longer exist as ordinances of common law (can. 6, 5).

Q. 182. What is the attitude of a religious who truly loves poverty?

A. The religious who truly loves poverty is always satisfied, in imitation of the apostle St. Paul, with the food and clothing provided. He never complains of the quantity or quality of the food or clothing given to him. As a poor man, he protects with every care that which he holds for his use. He sees to it that his needs are provided for at the least expense, and he is happy that sometimes he must suffer the lack of necessities.

Q. 183. On what can a religious profitably reflect to grow more in love with holy poverty?

A. To grow more in love with holy poverty the good religious can profitably reflect on the singular examples, among others, left us by our Lord Jesus Christ; on the rewards promised by Him to lovers of this virtue, and on the danger which quite frequently befalls him who trespasses against the vow, and lastly upon him who loves it too little, or who keeps it too negligently.

Chapter 12

The Vow of Chastity

Q. *184.* In what does the virtue of chastity consist?

A. The virtue of chastity is that virtue which guards us against acts of impurity, internal and external. Before God it would avail little to offer one's body, were it even physically virginal, if the soul were impure.

Q. *185.* How many kinds of chastity are there?

A. Chastity can be of three kinds:

1. conjugal chastity, which consists in abstaining from sensual pleasures except for those acts which the duties of matrimony impose on or permit married persons;

2. "vidual" chastity, that is of a widow or widower, which consists in the abstention from any sensual pleasure on the part of the surviving partner, although the pleasure had been enjoyed while the spouse was alive;

3. perfect chastity, which consists in the total abstention from any kind of sensual pleasure, even by those who could enjoy it since they are married. The abstention which was never interrupted by any voluntary act, in matrimony or out of it, is properly called virginity.

Q. *186.* What does the vow of chastity demand in the religious state?

A. It demands perfect chastity or at least that which is required of a widow and widower. Perfect virginity obviously is
one of the most beautiful adornments of life with which to
enter religion, but it is not absolutely required. The mind of
the Church on the point is clear. She encourages and prefers
her faithful to be virgins upon entering the religious state, but
she permits their entrance therein if they have lost the adornment of virginity provided they agree to be strictly chaste thereafter, by promise before profession and by vow after profession.

Q. *187.* Why is the vow of chastity required for the religious
state?

A. Because, as St. Thomas tells us, in the religious state it is
necessary to be free from all that which can prevent the total
dedication of oneself to the service of God. Now the use, even
licit, of sensual pleasures is an obstacle preventing a soul from
giving itself entirely to the service of God. This is true for two
reasons: first, because any use of sensual pleasure, by reason
of the vehemence of the pleasure, increases concupiscence, and
the soul is thereby held back from a perfect and exclusive seeking of God; secondly, because family cares, the responsibility
of looking after a husband or wife, of raising children, and of
administering the temporal goods of a household, necessarily
carry distractions. This is why St. Paul in his letter to the
Corinthians says: "He who is without a wife is solicitous (exclusively) for the things of God, how he might please the Lord;
he who has a wife is (necessarily) solicitous for the things of
the world, how he might please his wife" (I Cor. 7, 32, 33). For
this reason perpetual continence, that is, perfect chastity, no
less than poverty, is required for the essence of the religious
state.[15]

Q. *188.* What legal effects are produced by taking the vow of
chastity in a religious order?

[15] *Summa Theol.,* IIa–IIae, q. 186, a. 4.

A. It produces divers effects depending on whether the vow is simple or solemn.

Q. *189.* What legal effects are produced by taking a solemn vow of chastity in a religious order?

A. 1. It renders invalid any marriage attempted after the vow is taken (can. 579, 1073).

2. It breaks any promise or engagement to marry anyone no matter how valid the betrothal (can. 1017, 3); and in the particular case cited in canon 119, it can even dissolve a marriage contracted previous to the vow.

Q. *190.* What are the legal effects of a simple vow of chastity taken in a religious institute?

A. 1. It renders illicit, but not invalid, excepting the case of special privilege, any marriage which may be entered into after the vow is taken (can. 579, 1058).

2. It breaks any engagement to marry regardless of the validity of the contract (can. 1017, 3).

Q. *191.* How many sins are committed by one who violates the vow of chastity?

A. He commits two sins always: the sin of impurity and that of sacrilege.

A violation of the vow of chastity, forbidden by God, must be revealed to a confessor who may not know that such a vow binds his penitent.

Q. *192.* Why is the violation of the vow of chastity a sacrilege?

A. Because a sacrilege is the violation of a sacred thing. Indeed, he who has pronounced a vow of chastity in a religious institute approved by the Church, has offered to God, the Church assenting, his body and his soul; so that they become sacred things destined to honor God by means of the practice of perfect chastity. Therefore, failing in the vow, he truly violates a sacred thing and thus commits a sacrilege.

Q. *193.* Is every infraction by a religious of the virtue of chastity also an infraction of the vow?
A. Yes, because the extent of the matter of the vow is the same as the extent of the matter of the virtue, as we said above, Q. 191.

Q. *194.* Is the vow of chastity violated by acts which are only internal, such as deliberate thoughts and desires?
A. Yes, certainly, because the matter of the virtue of chastity is determined not only by the sixth, but also by the ninth commandment, which forbids even internal acts. As we said above, each violation of the virtue of this vow is a violation also of the vow.

Q. *195.* Do the sins, internal or external, which do not directly violate the virtue of chastity, but which constitute for it a danger, such as idle curiosity, particular friendships, etc., violate the vow?
A. We must distinguish. If these sins result in contracting also the malice of impurity, they certainly do violate the vow. If they remain free of this malice, being only imprudences, idle curiosities, and so on, they do not fall under the vow. However, they are always to be avoided more carefully since they carry great danger.

Q. *196.* Does the vow of chastity, whether it be solemn or simple, admit of lightness of matter?
A. Of itself it does not admit of lightness of matter since the virtue of chastity itself does not admit of any lightness. It is understood, however, that one does not commit a mortal sin against this beautiful virtue without full knowledge and full consent of the will.

Q. 197. Can an act which seems to be only a venial sin for a person in the world become mortal for a religious?

A. Yes it can, because of the scandal that may be given.

Q. 198. What are the punishments sanctioned by the Church for religious who violate this vow?

A. 1. The religious who, having a solemn vow of chastity, attempts to contract matrimony incurs *ipso facto,* that is, immediately by that very fact, excommunication reserved simply to the Holy See. The same holds for the accomplice who attempts to enter into marriage with that religious (can. 2388, 1).

2. The professed of simple perpetual vows who contracts marriage incurs the excommunication *latae sententiae,* i.e., of automatic excommunication reserved to the ordinary. The same holds true for the accomplice, no matter who the person is, who enters into marriage with that religious (can. 2388, 2).

3. Finally, religious bound by whatever kind of vows, even temporary ones, who attempt or in any way contract marriage, though it be only civil, are irregular (can. 985, 3).

Q. 199. What are the blessings that flow from the faithful observance of the vow of chastity?

A. We may cite them as follows:

1. St. Paul tells us that through chaste living the religious is freed from the care of the world and of a family. His only concern on earth is how to please the Lord; his heart, therefore, is not divided in its affections (I Cor. 5, 33).

2. Through chaste living he lives on earth in the manner in which angels live in heaven. Our Lord said: "Blessed are the clean of heart for they shall see God" (Matt. 5, 9). He is in complete control of self and he enjoys that peace which transcends everything here below.

3. Through chaste living he ordinarily acquires, like Mary, a spiritual paternity or maternity, much more desirable than any other form of earthly paternity or maternity, so that his

zeal and his words to others acquire a character and a power all their own.

4. Finally, chaste living singularly honors the Holy Catholic Church and our Mother, before whom this beautiful virtue of chastity, particularly as it is practiced by her male and female religious, becomes her dearest and most precious adornment, her crowning glory.

Q. *200.* How must chastity be guarded by a religious?
A. A virtue so precious and delicate as chastity must be guarded by a religious with the utmost care and diligence. Therefore, in all his actions he must pay attention to "little things," but especially in guarding this particular virtue. He who guards well his chastity is made comparable to the angels, but he who violates it is made abominable before God.

Q. *201.* Chiefly by what means must chastity be guarded?
A. By observing scrupulously the rules of Christian modesty; by loving and practicing mortification; by cultivating a true spirit of prayer and a great devotion to Our Lady, the Queen and special protector of virginal hearts.

~~~~~~

Chapter 13

The Vow of Obedience

~~~~~~

Q. 202. In what does the vow of obedience consist?

A. The vow of obedience made in religion consists of "the promise made to God to obey one's legitimate superiors in all things which directly or indirectly refer to religious observance in conformity with the particular rule and constitutions."

Q. 203. Why is it said that the vow of obedience is a promise made to God?

A. Because, although the persons to whom the religious makes submission are the legitimate superiors of his institute, the promise indeed is not made to them but to God, and in this we find the essence of the vow.

Q. 204. Why do religious take this vow of obedience?

A. Because the vow of obedience pertains to the essence of the religious state (can. 487).

Q. 205. How is it proved that the vow of obedience pertains to the essence of the religious state?

A. The religious state is a certain discipline or practical method of tending to perfection. Whoever, then, is in the condition of having to receive instruction or of being guided in a definite action so as to reach this end, needs to be under the discipline of him who is deputed to instruct and familiarize him in the way that leads to the fixed end, as a disciple under the leadership of his master. This is why religious, in those things which concern the practice of the religious life, have the need of being under him who instructs and leads them. Now the virtue which facilitates this subjection to another's instruction and leadership is called obedience. Wherefore, obedience is necessary for religious perfection, that is, for the religious state.

This conclusion St. Thomas confirms with this reasoning:

Religious perfection essentially consists in the imitation of Jesus Christ, for we read: "If thou wilt be perfect, come follow Me" (Matt. 19, 20). Now among the virtues principally evident in the life of Jesus Christ is obedience, as St. Paul shows: "He was obedient, even unto death" (Phil. 2, 8). It is therefore evident that obedience pertains to the perfection, or more exactly, to the essence of the religious life.[16]

Q. *206.* What authority has the superior by virtue of the religious profession?

A. There comes to him a twofold authority, the first based on the virtue of obedience, the second on the vow of obedience.

Insofar as the professed religious agrees to become a member of a religious society or family, he acknowledges in the superior the authority to command as a father and head of the religious family to which he belongs. Hence as a good son, he owes obedience to the head of the religious family even if there were no vow.

Further, inasmuch as the religious takes the vow of obedience, he recognizes in the superior a special authority to command him in virtue of the same vow which he voluntarily made.

Q. *207.* What legal effects does the vow of obedience produce?

[16] *Summa theol.,* IIa–IIae, q. 186, a. 5.

A. It produces several legal effects depending on whether the vow is simple or solemn.

Q. 208. What legal effect does the solemn vow of obedience produce?
A. The solemn vow of obedience renders the person bound by such a vow incapable of contracting any new personal obligation burdensome to the religious life without the consent of his legitimate superior (can. 579). Wherefore, not only may the superior cancel such obligations but, by virtue of canon 579, they are *ipso facto* null and void.

Q. 209. What is meant by this burdensome obligation?
A. By it is meant an obligation which obstructs or in any other way impedes the regular development of the religious life either in reference to the community or to the individual himself who made the vow.

Q. 210. What legal effects does a simple vow of obedience produce?
A. A simple vow of obedience taken in religion renders voidable by the superior all obligations onerous for religious living which have been contracted by a person bound by this kind of vow (can. 1312, 1).

Q. 211. What is meant by the phrase, "voidable by the superior" as to onerous obligations contracted?
A. It means that the obligations are not of themselves null and void, but that the superior can make them null and void.

Q. 212. Why are such obligations voidable without being from the start null and void?
A. Because one of the notable differences between a simple and solemn vow is precisely this: that the solemn vow renders one bound by such a vow incapable of contracting any kind of personal obligation onerous to the religious life, since

through his vow he has consecrated to God not only the exercise of his will, but even the will itself; as in the vow of poverty he gave up not only the use of temporal goods but even the very right to possess them. In the simple vow of obedience, on the other hand, he has promised God only the exercise of his will, and this within the limits prescribed in the quasi-contract which by profession comes into being between the professed and his institute. Accordingly, the superior can cancel, that is, refuse to recognize any obligation made after the profession by his subject, if he judges the obligation out of harmony with prior obligations assumed by the profession. However, until the superior does actually cancel them, the religious professed of simple vows must fulfill the obligations contracted, since of themselves they are valid. For example, if a religious of simple vows promises to recite the rosary daily, and the superior, fully aware of it, does not forbid it, the religious is obliged to keep the promise (see Q. 134).

Q. 213. Who are the legitimate superiors whom the religious is obliged to obey?

A. They are the proper superiors of the institute to which the religious belongs, not excluding the Supreme Pontiff to whom every religious owes obedience, not only as a Christian, but even as a religious by virtue of the vow of obedience (can. 499, 1).

Q. 214. Are religious obliged in virtue of the vow to obey even the bishops?

A. 1. If in the formula of profession, as some have it, obedience is vowed not only to the proper superiors but also to the bishop, evidently then there is contracted the obligation of obeying the bishop even by force of the vow. The same obedience is due to the bishop if the constitutions so enjoin it even though there is no mention of it in the formula of profession.

2. In the other cases it is not easy to say whether the obliga-

tion to obey the bishop is due only in virtue of his jurisdiction
over all in his diocese, including religious, or also by reason
of the vow.

Those who hold the opinion that it is by force of the vow
base their arguments on a certain parallel between the pope
and the bishop. To the pope, they say, because of canon 469, 1,
obedience is due by all religious in virtue of their vow; hence,
in the orbit of his own jurisdiction it is due in the same way
to the bishop, particularly if the institute is of diocesan law.

Those who hold the opposite view, namely, that obedience
is not due to the bishop by virtue of the vow, argue thus: The
obedience to be given by religious in virtue of the vow extends
only as far as is promised in the profession. Now it is understood by the expressed will of the Church in the Code that
religious owe obedience to the pope by virtue of the vow, but
there is no mention made of the bishop in this regard. Hence
the bishop is excluded from this consideration. This second
opinion seems to be preferable.

Q. *215.* Must women religious obey the regular superiors of
their order?

A.   If the women religious are exempt and placed under the
jurisdiction of the regular superiors of the order to which they
belong, they must certainly obey in virtue of their vow in all
those things over which the regular superiors have jurisdiction in conformity with common law and their own constitutions. If they are not exempt the vow does not oblige them to
obey the regular superiors of their order, save in particular
cases. With reference to sisters, it is expressly forbidden by the
Code for the regular superiors of the order to govern female
religious congregations without special apostolic indult, although the sisters are members of that order.

Q. *216.* May a superior in virtue of the vow of obedience
order his religious subject to obey in all things?

A.   No. He can command only in those things which directly or indirectly have to do with religious observance in conformity with the rule and constitutions. This is clearly stated in the very formula of profession.

Q. *217.* What then is the proper matter of the vow of obedience?

A. The proper matter of the vow of obedience embraces the commands and precepts of the superiors, which are in conformity directly or even indirectly with the rule and constitutions professed (see Q. 56). In the formula of profession obedience is promised to the superiors "in conformity with the rule and constitutions."

Q. *218.* Do the particular prescriptions of the rule and constitutions fall under the vow of obedience?

A. No, only the commands and precepts of the legitimate superiors constitute the proper object of the vow, not the constitutions in their reference to the doing or nondoing of anything. These either do not oblige in conscience, as is true in many institutes, or, if they do so oblige, yet they cannot be said to be proper objects or matter of the vow.

Q. *219.* Why is it said that the proper objects or matter of the vow of obedience are the commands or precepts of the superior in conformity directly or indirectly with the rule and constitutions?

A. Because it is not always necessary for a thing to be explicitly contained in the rule and constitutions for it to be a proper object of command by the superiors. It is enough that it be there implicitly, which is true when it furthers at least indirectly the objectives of the religious life in general or of the particular institute.

Q. *220.* Is a religious obliged to obey a command of his superior when he doubts whether or not it is conformable to the rule?

A. Yes, for when there is a doubt in the mind of the religious subject, the judgment of the superior is to prevail.

Q. 221. Would it be against the vow of obedience to make any contradictory observations to a commanding superior?

A. In itself, no. Indeed, on occasions, when it is a question of calling to his attention a grave inconvenience to oneself or to another, there is an obligation to remonstrate. However, so as not to give the impression of lacking in obedience on these occasions, a religious, over and above the right intention, should have the disposition in his soul to obey if the superior insists despite the observation. Furthermore, the remonstrance, besides being well-founded and reasonable, should be advanced with the greatest humility and respect.

Q. 222. Does he who obeys against his will and against his own conviction sin against the vow?

A. He does not sin against the vow because the command of the superior, which is the object of the vow, is obeyed freely. However, the religious deprives himself of the greater merit of obedience done with good will and, as far as is humanly possible, with detachment from his own judgment.

Q. 223. Why is it said, "with detachment from his own judgment"; and, "so far as is humanly possible"?

A. Because it is certainly praiseworthy to seek in acts of obedience, to conform one's own judgment or viewpoint to that of the commanding superior. Of course, this is not demanded absolutely by the vow or even by the virtue of obedience. Sometimes the personal conviction against that which the superior commands can be so strong that it cannot be dislodged. For this reason it cannot be said that if the order is obeyed it is badly obeyed. Indeed, it might even be of greater merit inasmuch as it requires greater will power to obey. The surrender of one's personal opinions is not an essential element of the virtue or of the vow of obedience.

Q. 224. Does the vow of obedience admit of smallness of matter?

A. Yes. Both the virtue and the vow of obedience admit of smallness of matter. Both are susceptible to modification in gravity depending on whether the matter to be observed is grave or light. It is to be noted, however, that the matter of obedience can become grave either in itself, as when one is commanded to go from one house to another, or in its attending circumstances, as when one is forbidden to look out of a window, on account of the great danger to the religious life of him who is so commanded.

Q. 225. Is it always a mortal sin, then, when one fails against the vow of obedience in grave matter?

A. Not always, for even when the matter is grave, there are required for mortal sin against the vow of obedience full advertence and deliberate consent. Further, the superior must will to bind one gravely. There is no contradiction in the fact that the superior even in grave things may oblige the subject only lightly, that is, under venial sin. Only a formal precept always obliges gravely (see Q. 60).

Q. 226. In practice how can one know whether or not the superior in commanding binds one under pain of mortal sin?

A. In practice a command is known to bind under mortal sin or not from the manner in which it is given. For example, when the superior says he is commanding "in virtue of the Holy Spirit and of holy obedience," or "under formal precept." These and similar expressions clearly indicate that the command is given under grave obligation or pain of mortal sin.

Safe and excellent guides in this matter are the constitutions in which ordinarily are determined the conditions necessary before the superior can, in act or intent, command in virtue of the vow of obedience under grave obligation or pain of mortal sin. Thus, in the constitutions of the Dominican Order there is a prescription that the precepts of the superior, in order to oblige one under mortal sin and in virtue of the vow, must be conveyed by determined formula, namely: "We order you in virtue of holy obedience." Likewise, in the constitutions of the Jesuits it is prescribed that whenever the superior uses words which indicate a command, such as, "I will it, I command that this be done," it is never intended that these words imply a grave obligation to obey if there is not also added the formula, "In the name of our Lord Jesus Christ," or, "In virtue of holy obedience."

Q. 227. What, then, in religion, is a formal precept?
A. As we said above, Q. 59, it is the expressed command of the superior commanding in virtue of the vow of obedience with the intention of binding a subject gravely, that is, under serious obligation in conscience to do or to omit doing a certain thing.

Q. 228. Have all the superiors this power of commanding "in virtue of holy obedience," that is, imposing a formal precept?
A. No. This power rests only with those to whom it is given by the laws of the Church or by the particular constitutions, and only in the manner authorized.

Q. 229. Then do the commands of legitimate superiors always oblige in conscience or do they oblige only when they are given under formal precept?
A. The true commands of superiors always oblige both by reason of the vow and of the virtue of obedience (see Q. 202). When there is no formal precept, even if the matter is grave, superiors may oblige one only venially if that be their pleasure; likewise, when such is the customary interpretation, these commands bind only under venial fault. But when the formal precept is given, then the obligation to obey is always grave, and it cannot become light except through lack of advertence or full consent of the will (Q. 60).

Q. 230. How many sins are committed in the violation of the vow of obedience?

A. A violation of the vow of obedience, as we said in reference to the vow of chastity, always carries a twofold specific malice, namely, one sin against the virtue of obedience and another against the virtue of religion. Against the virtue of religion inasmuch as it breaks a promise made to God; and against the virtue of obedience inasmuch as the religious, abstracting even from his vow, is obliged to show himself respectful and subject to the commands of his legitimate superiors precisely because they are his superiors.

Q. 231. Can a religious fail in the virtue of obedience without failing against the vow?

A. In certain cases he can, since the object of the virtue of obedience is in itself much more extensive than the object of the vow, be it solemn or simple. For example, a religious is obliged to obey the legitimate civil authority which governs a nation, not because of the vow, but simply because of ordinary or common obedience, as St. Paul says: "Obey your prelates" (Heb. 13, 17). Wherefore, if a religious disobeys any one of these civil superiors he fails in the virtue of obedience, but not in the vow (Q. 119).

Q. 232. Is it true that the vow of obedience is the most excellent of the three vows of religion?

A. It is most certainly true. In the vow of poverty one renounces temporal goods, which indeed pertain to man but only as things extraneous to his person. With the vow of chastity one renounces something more intimate pertaining to his person, yet which does not go beyond sensual pleasures. With the vow of obedience, however, one gives up his own will surrendering it to legitimate superiors in many things. Now liberty and one's free will are goods much more excellent and much more precious than any other good, temporal or corporal. Further, the object of the religious vow of obedience is more extensive, as we shall now see, than the objects of the other two vows. Since the religious in promising obedience to his legitimate superiors in conformity with the rule of his institute necessarily agrees to live in conformity with the rule, which always includes as its essential elements the vows of poverty and chastity, he obliges himself to all the duties of the religious life. This is why in the formula of profession of several religious orders, for example, the Dominicans, only the vow of obedience is expressly mentioned, for in taking it one intends to take all the three vows of religion.

Q.   233. What penalties does a disobedient religious incur?
A.   No penalty is actually determined in the Code for the violation of the vow of obedience. Ordinarily the penalties for it are determined by the constitutions of each religious institute. Further, superiors, having the right to command by force of the vow and by the virtue of obedience (Q. 58), can themselves fix the penalties either before or after the transgression. Indeed, even the punishment itself can be imposed, if that seems opportune, as an obedience.

Chapter 14

~~~~~~

The Religious Profession

~~~~~~

Q. 234. What is profession in the religious state?

A. Profession in its broad meaning is "any public avowal to practice some form of the perfect life conformable with rules lawfully approved." In this sense even the tertiaries of a religious order are said to make profession in its third order.

Strictly speaking, however, by religious profession is meant the public pronouncing of vows. These vows, to be valid, must be public and must be pronounced not in any manner, but in that form which the constitutions of each institute prescribe (Q. 118).

Q. 235. Why does a religious profession properly speaking assume the nature of a contract?

A. Since the religious profession is made with the consent of the superiors of the institute, it binds both parties, the institute and the one making profession (can. 572, 1). It obliges the professed to the observance of the rule and the vows, and it obliges the religious institute to accord to the professed all those rights and duties which, according to the rules of the institute, befit him. It thus assumes the nature of a bilateral contract (Q. 124).

Q. 236. How many kinds of religious profession are there?
A. A religious profession may be either simple or solemn. It is simple when only simple vows are taken, solemn when solemn vows are taken (can. 574, 1; Q. 128).

Q. 237. Is there another classification of professions?
A. Yes, the profession also may be temporary or perpetual. It is temporary when the vows are taken for a limited period of time, as for one year, three years, five years; it is perpetual when the vows are taken for the rest of one's earthly life, that is, till death (can. 574; Q. 123).

A simple profession may be temporary or perpetual, while a solemn profession is always and necessarily perpetual by its very nature (Q. 263).

Q. 238. To whom does it belong to admit a religious to profession?
A. The legitimate superiors of a religious institute have the right to admit one to profession with the consent of the council or chapter in accordance with their constitutions (can. 572, 1).

We are not speaking here of the pronouncement of the vows, which of course is made by the one taking the vows, but of the right of the superiors, through an inquiry made as to the fitness of novices, to permit them to take the vows (Q. 242, 1).

The vote of the council or chapter is decisive when it concerns the first profession. When it concerns the simple perpetual or solemn profession it is only consultative (can. 575, 2). The legitimate superior makes the final decision in these cases.

Q. 239. What other actions must precede the taking of vows?
A. All professions, simple or solemn, to be made by religious women must be preceded by a canonical examination (Q. 86), as was true of their admittance into the novitiate (can. 552, 2).

For all, both men and women, a course of spiritual exercises of at least eight full days is required.

Q. 240. Are the spiritual exercises required only before the first profession or each time that the vows are renewed?
A. Strictly interpreting the Code it seems that the spiritual exercises are required only before the first profession, for the canon cited speaks only of a novice who is to take vows, which means a first profession. For successive renewals of profession, the Code simply states that "the religious profession should be renewed in conformity with the prescriptions of the particular constitutions."

At all events, whether the constitutions prescribe spiritual exercises before the making of any profession or whether they do not, it is clear according to the spirit of the Code and the nature of the act that at least a brief retreat should precede any religious profession.

Q. 241. Is there an obligation to make a will before the first profession?
A. When one is to take first vows in a congregation of simple vows, a will has to be made beforehand (can. 569, 3). For those who will proceed to solemn vows after their first profession, as do nuns and regulars, it is only advised.

Q. 242. What conditions are required for a valid profession?
A. For a valid profession, in conformity with canon 572, the following conditions are required:
1. The legitimate age, that is, sixteen completed years for temporary profession, twenty-one completed years for perpetual profession whether simple or solemn. The year must be computed in accordance with the norm laid down by canon 34, 3, 3. Thus the profession cannot be made till the day after the birthday anniversary which completes the required number of years.

2. The novitiate validly made, that is, having verified all the requirements canonically laid down for it (Q. 84 ff.). It is not necessary for the profession to be made immediately upon the termination of the novitiate. For good reasons it can be delayed a month or two, but not indefinitely since there must be a moral union with profession. The novitiate by its nature is not only a probation but a preparation for profession.

3. The temporary profession of at least three years must precede before one can be admitted to perpetual profession simple or solemn (can. 574, 1; Q. 290).

4. The consent of the legitimate superiors, according to the norms of the proper constitutions.

Who these superiors are and in what manner they are to express their consent must be determined by the constitutions of each religious institute. The Code merely notes that "there is required the vote of the council or of the chapter," and that this vote for the first profession is decisive, while for any renewing profession it is only consultative (can. 575, 2). Consequently, a superior cannot validly admit to a first profession anyone who has been disapproved by the council or chapter, while he may, as far as validity goes, admit one to a renewal of profession, temporary, perpetual, simple or solemn, even if the council or chapter has voted against it. This of course would be imprudent to do except in exceptional cases.

5. The profession must be pronounced freely, without any fear or deceit. Whoever, notwithstanding his rank, in any manner forces a person to take vows, simple or solemn, temporary or perpetual, incurs immediate excommunication (can. 2352).

6. The profession must be spoken, that is, the one making profession must expressly declare what he is professing. Hence a tacit or presumed profession, as for example, if an unprofessed novice were to continue living in religion as if professed, without having explicitly made profession, it would not be valid today, though at one time it was considered valid.

7. The profession must be accepted by the legitimate superior or by his delegate. Who this legitimate superior actually

is the Code does not specify, hence it must be left to the constitutions of each institute to determine the official.

There are religious institutes in which vows are taken but the profession is not made before the superior nor accepted by him, as in the institutes of the Daughters of Saint Vincent de Paul, wherein the sisters make the three vows of poverty, chastity, and obedience only to God. Strictly speaking these institutes do not belong to the category of true religious institutes but of pious unions or societies of persons living in common in the manner of religious, as the secular institutes (Q. 26).

Q. 243. How can a profession which was invalid become valid?

A. If the religious profession was invalid through any external impediment, for example, made before the completion of sixteen years of age, to rectify it recourse must be made to the Holy See, or the impediment having been revealed, the profession is renewed when the proper age has been attained (can. 586, 1). Since the promulgation of the Code the case of a tacit profession, wherein one continues to live, even for a long time, in religion as one validly professed has been excluded from being a mode of rectification.

If, on the other hand, the profession was invalid due to lack of internal consent, then "to rectify it, it is sufficient to renew it with a true consent, provided that in the meantime the acceptance of it on the part of the religious has not been recalled" (can. 586, 2). For example, if a novice while making profession, though he pronounces with his lips the formula of profession nevertheless maliciously does not give his internal consent, the profession is without doubt null and void. To rectify it, however, there is no obligation on his part to ask for a dispensation or even to reveal it to others, except to his confessor. All he has to do, provided that in the meantime it is not apparent that his superiors have recalled their consent, is interiorly to give his true consent, and the profession without further ado becomes valid.

Q. 244. What is to be done in the case of a well-founded doubt as to the validity of the profession, when the religious in question does not wish to renew his profession for the sake of certainty nor to apply for rectification?

A. The case should be referred to the Holy See (can. 586, 3).

It is not lawful for the religious nor for the institute to remain in doubt concerning the validity of the profession. When a well-founded doubt arises, depending on the case, the procedure is first to try to get a renewal of the profession from the subject, then to apply for rectification for the sake of certainty from the Holy See, or to expose the case to the Holy See so that it can examine and determine what is to be done in the matter.

Q. 245. If a novice falls gravely ill and is in danger of death, can he be admitted to profession even if he has not as yet completed his year of novitiate?

A. Yes, he can be admitted; indeed, it is praiseworthy to allow him to make profession. He then enjoys all the indulgences, privileges, and suffrages of his institute, and above all these a plenary indulgence in the form of jubilee. However, should he afterwards recover, such a profession made in danger of death no longer has any effect. When the time required for his novitiate has been completed, he should again make his profession, observing all the formalities and conditions as if he had never been professed (The Sacred Congregation of Religious, December 30, 1922).

Q. 246. What obligations follow one's religious profession over and above the observance of the vows?

A. Two fundamental obligations follow:

1. the obligation to tend to perfection;

2. the obligation to acknowledge the superiors of the order or congregation as his proper superiors and to obey them not only by reason of the vow when it obliges him but also by reason of the virtue of obedience inasmuch as every subject is

obliged to render obedience to his legitimate superiors whether he is bound by vow or not (Q. 229).

The religious profession, as we have said above, Q. 235, is a bilateral contract between the religious institute and the professed. The institute is obliged to accord to the professed the right to religious life with all the rights which it implies, while the professed contracts the obligation to live according to the rule he has professed to obey and to acknowledge the superiors of the institute as his own.

Q. 247. Does there also arise for religious after their profession the obligation to remain in the institute so chosen?

A. There does necessarily arise a strict obligation to remain in the institute of one's profession for the period of time promised in the vow (can. 593).

Indeed, as we have said above, Q. 235, the profession is a kind of bilateral contract which carries with it a strict obligation for both parties. Each religious has the duty to correspond and persevere in that vocation to which he has been called by God (I Cor. 7, 20).

Q. 248. May a professed religious be a godfather or godmother in baptism or confirmation?

A. No, a professed religious may not be a sponsor in these sacraments without special permission from the Holy See (can. 766, 4; 706, 3).

Q. 249. May a professed religious continue to be a member of a third order secular?

A. No. However, should the religious become free of vows for any reason and return to the world, his or her membership in a third order revives without any other formality.

Q. 250. Why is a religious profession, and particularly the solemn profession, called a second baptism?

A. Because a religious profession produces three effects simi-

lar to those of baptism, namely, it frees one from all temporal
punishment due to sin, it makes the old man die to the world,
and it gives birth to a new life.

The freedom from temporal punishment due to sin accrues
to him by reason of the oblation of the religious, particularly
in a solemn profession, which he makes of self to God. God
grants a remission of all punishment due to sin. This is common doctrine, taught by all theologians following the lead of
St. Thomas (IV *Sent.,* d. IV, q. 3, a. 3). What act, indeed, could
be more expiating than such an offering? Were a religious in
the state of grace to die immediately after his profession, he
would promptly be admitted into heaven.

It makes the man die to the world because by profession the
religious dies to the world and to all its concupiscences. He
lives apart from the world so definitely that in days past the
religous profession brought about a kind of civic death. He
remains hidden, as St. Paul puts it and is buried in Christ
(Rom. 6, 4).

Finally, it gives the religious a birth to a new life. This is
evident by the fact that new thoughts, new feelings, new tastes,
and new orientation, new labors, and new methods of doing
things attend the religious after profession, so much so that
it can be said of him that which the Council of Trent says of
the newly baptized, namely, "that they walk no longer according to the flesh, but stripped of the old man, they become pure
innocents, without spot, dear to God" in all the manifestations
of their new life (Session V, on Original Sin, 5).

Q. *251.* Where must a religious profession be registered?
A. A simple profession, whether of temporary or perpetual
vows, should be registered in the profession book which is kept
in the archives of the convent or monastery (can. 576, 2). A
solemn profession is registered in the same professional book
and also is to be recorded in the baptismal book of the parish
where the religious was baptized (can. 576, 2). The superior
who receives the solemn profession of one of his subjects has

the obligation of sending notice of it to the parish priest where the subject had been baptized (can. 576, 2).

The parish priest who receives such a notice is obliged to register the profession in the baptismal book (can. 470, 2).

Chapter 15

~~~~~~

The Simple Profession

~~~~~~

Q. 252. When is a profession said to be simple?
A. That profession is simple in which one takes only simple vows (Q. 128).

Before the sixteenth century a simple temporary profession was unknown. In all religious institutes of men or women only a solemn or at least a simple perpetual profession was made (Q. 262).

Q. 253. Is a simple profession always temporary?
A. No, it can be perpetual, depending on whether the vows taken are temporary or perpetual (Q. 123).

Q. 254. What age is required for a first profession?
A. The first religious profession, which must be simple and temporary, under pain of invalidity, cannot be made before the completion of the sixteenth year of age (can. 573).

The years are reckoned according to the norm of canon 34, 3, 3. Consequently, the profession cannot be made before the day following the sixteenth anniversary of one's birth.

Q. 255. When is a simple profession necessarily required?
A. A simple temporary profession is necessarily required as

a step toward solemn profession or to a simple perpetual one. "A simple temporary profession must always precede a perpetual profession of simple vows or of solemn vows" (see Qq. 264, 290).[17]

Q. 256. What are the legal effects of a simple profession?
A. A simple profession, temporary or perpetual, always produces the following effects:

1. It renders illicit all acts opposed to the vows pronounced (can. 579). They are illicit, but not invalid, "unless the contrary is expressed in the constitutions approved by the Church," that is, where there is explicit mention made in the constitutions that although the vows are simple all acts performed by members of this institute contrary to the vows are not only illicit but invalid as well.

Consequently, in accordance with canon law any marriage contracted by a religious professed of simple vows, and during the time of the obligation of the vows, is illicit but nevertheless valid. A gift made of one's own goods without the permission of the superior is illicit, yet valid; and the same is to be said of other contracts made.

The Church can, by approving the constitutions of a religious institute, regard also as invalid all acts opposed to the vows of one simply professed, but the constitutions in question must provide for that very clearly. An example of this is the case of the Jesuits, for in that Society, by the expressed will of the Church, a member with simple vows not only illicitly but also invalidly contracts marriage.

2. Concerning one's own temporal goods, the professed of simple vows, during the time of the obligation of the vows, can keep, unless his constitutions determine otherwise, proprietorship over them and is capable of acquiring other goods (can. 580, 1), although he may not administer them. Before his profession he must turn over the administration of his goods to another for all the period of the obligation of his vows

[17] Can. 574, a. 1.

(can. 569, 1). If his particular constitutions do not regulate otherwise, or if he has not obtained a special permission from the Holy See, he may not even use them to his own advantage, but before his profession he must freely make provision to turn over to someone the use and fruits of these goods (can. 569, 1).

Q. 257. May the religious after profession, with vows still in force, change the arrangements for the administration of his goods?
A. He may, but not of his own free will. He has to obtain the permission of his superior general; or, in the case of a nun, the permission of the ordinary of the place, and if her monastery is subject to the regular superior, his permission is also required (can. 580, 3). Excepted is the case when the change in notable part at least is to be made in favor of the institute. In this event it is necessary to obtain the permission of the Holy See for the change to be effected.

Q. 258. May the religious of simple vows, during the term of his vows, change his will made before profession?
A. He may not without the permission of the Holy See. If the case is urgent, he must have the permission of his own major superior If this is not possible, then the permission of his local superior suffices (can. 583, 2).

Q. 259. To whom do goods belong which are acquired by a professed religious even of simple vows either by his own personal industry or in line with religious work?
A. They belong to the institute (can. 580, 2).
It appears from this that a professed religious, should he leave the institute after the term of his vows expires or is dispensed from them, or should he even become a fugitive or apostate from religion, has no right to any compensation for any work done while in religion, no matter what was the nature of the work done and no matter how advantageous to the institute were his labors.

Q. *260.* May a religious of simple vows freely give up proprietorship of his goods?

A. During the time he remains professed he may not do it without special permission. It is stated emphatically in canon 583, 1: "It is not lawful for professed of simple vows, even if they are perpetual, to surrender the dominion of their personal property of their own accord by an act to be executed during the lifetime of the religious making the surrender."

Q. *261.* At the expiration of vows and before renewing them, may a religious change his mind either concerning his will or concerning the administration of his goods?

A. He may not, for once he has made the vows, even temporary ones, there is no moment given him in which he can be considered without vows, since if he wishes to remain in religion he must renew them without any interval elapsing (can. 577, 1).

Chapter 16

The Solemn Profession

Q. 262. When is a profession said to be solemn?
A. That profession is said to be solemn in which one takes solemn vows (Q. 128).

The real difference between a simple and solemn profession is not to be found in the external ceremonies of each no matter how elaborate or solemn they may be, but in the nature of the vows one takes.

Q. 263. Can a solemn profession be temporary?
A. It can never be temporary. By its very nature it is perpetual (Q. 237).

Q. 264. Can solemn profession be made immediately after the novitiate?
A. Today, it cannot, although formerly it was done. A simple profession of temporary vows at least of three years must now precede solemn profession (Qq. 255, 290).

Q. 265. Why is this so today?
A. Because in olden times only a solemn profession was recognized as fitting for all religious. In that period, then, immediately after the novitiate one took solemn vows without any other formality (Q. 252).

Q. *266.* What age is required for the making of a solemn profession?

A. Solemn profession may not be made unless one has completed twenty-one years of age (can. 572, 1, 1).

Therefore, although the Code requires only a three-year period of simple profession, if the religious who is simply professed upon the expiration of these three years has not as yet reached twenty-one years of age, he cannot make his solemn profession. It is for this reason that the Code itself declares that the first profession that has to precede the solemn or perpetual one should last for three years at least, and longer if the age of twenty-one required for the solemn profession is not reached at the end of the three-year period of simple vows. Thus, if a novice makes his first profession at the age of sixteen, the period of his simple vows will not be only for three years but until he reaches the age of twenty-one (see Q. 242 for the correct computation of age).

Q. *267.* Is a canonical examination required before a solemn profession?

A. It is required only for religious women (see Qq. 85, 86, 87).

Q. *268.* What legal effects does a solemn profession produce?

A. A solemn profession renders not only illicit but invalid any act contrary to the vows (can. 579).

Thus a marriage attempted by a religious with solemn vows is null and void. A contract to buy or sell without permission of the superiors is null and void, and a vow onerous to the obligations of the religious life likewise is null and void.

Q. *269.* With reference to temporal goods, what legal effects has a solemn profession?

A. With reference to temporal goods, a religious with solemn vows gives up not only the administration, use, and fruits of them, but even the proprietorship of them (Q. 156). For this reason:

1. Before his solemn profession, and precisely within the immediate sixty days that precede it, a religious, save for a particular indult or permission obtained from the Holy See, must "renounce in favor of whomever he pleases all the temporal goods actually in his possession, on condition of his profession subsequently taking place" (can. 581, 1). When the profession actually has been made, then "there arises the further obligation of seeing to it as soon as possible that the conveyance of ownership to another be rendered civilly legal and binding."

2. After the solemn profession, all goods and revenues accruing to him from whatever source, by heritage, inheritance, gift, or the like, and of which he has not lawfully disposed before his profession, will belong to the religious order in which he has made profession, if the order is capable of possessing goods. This procedure will prevail unless a special indult has been obtained from the Holy See (can. 582, 1). If the order is incapable of possessing goods, their ownership passes to the Holy See. The use and administration of the goods, however, will remain in the hands of the order according to its rule and constitution (Q. 31).

Among the religious orders of men which are incapable of possessing temporal goods as their own, particularly real estate, are the Capuchins. We do not know of any institute of nuns which cannot possess such goods. Indeed, it is formally prescribed that each nun bring in her dowry which is then retained and administered by her monastery (Q. 85, 5).

Q. 270. Can a religious, before his solemn profession, renounce in favor of another person not only the goods which he actually possessed at the time but also those which he might possibly later inherit? For example, if the religious does not actually own anything at the time of his profession but expects a legacy from his parents or other relatives, can he from the moment of his profession renounce these expected goods?

A. We must first distinguish three cases of future sources of temporal wealth:

1. Goods which come to a religious with solemn vows after his profession by reason of his own personal industry or by reason of the institute of which he is a member. He cannot make any renunciation of these expected goods, since they do not belong to him but to his order (can. 580, 2).

2. Goods which are in the realm of pure possibility; that is, at the time of the profession there exists no knowledge that such revenue may accrue and no reasonable hope that some day one may come into possession of goods. He cannot make a renunciation of goods neither owned nor reasonably expected, and which being improbable in themselves could only come through the remotest sort of possibility.

3. Goods in which there is a well-founded hope that one day the religious will come into possession of them, not because he is a religious, but because of family ties whence the goods would come to him by the normal and legal mode of inheritance, may be renounced before the profession. While at the time of profession the religious does not own the goods, his chance of future possession is so well-founded that a definite legal right—a right of estimable price and value—accrues to him, and it is this right that can be renounced at the time of the profession. There is a custom in some religious orders to permit, and even to demand this kind of renunciation, particularly when it is clearly foreseen that a legacy will come to the religious after the death of his parents or other near relatives (see Dominican Constitutions, 115).

Q. 271. Is there always the equal obligation of making a civil renunciation as well?

A. Ordinarily, so that the deed be not impeded in perfect

execution, the Church obliges the religious to make the renunciation civilly binding as well (can. 581, 1). In special circumstances prudence may counsel doing otherwise, in which
case the Holy See can grant a dispensation.

Chapter 17

The Temporary Profession

Q. 272. When is a profession said to be temporary?
A. That profession is temporary "which, at the end of the novitiate, is made by a novice taking his vows not for life but for a definite period of time, as for one year, three years, five years, and so on" (Q. 123).

Q. 273. Is a temporary profession simple or solemn?
A. A temporary profession is necessarily simple, for as we said above, Q. 263, only a solemn profession is of its nature perpetual.

Q. 274. For what period of time can one make a temporary profession?
A. It can be made for any period of time, according to the constitutions of each religious institute, as long as it is not "for always" or "till death." It will remain temporary although it be constantly renewed and even should this continue for life (Q. 22).

Q. 275. When is the temporary profession obligatory?
A. The temporary profession is always obligatory before the taking of perpetual vows, simple or solemn (can. 574, 1; Qq. 264, 290).

It is to be noted that if a religious bound by perpetual vows passes from one order to another, for example, from the Franciscan to the Dominican, he can, after completing his novitiate in the Dominican Order immediately make perpetual profession—solemn in this case, or simple perpetual if he passed to a congregation—without having to make a temporary one before the perpetual profession (can. 634).

Q. 276. How long must a simple temporary profession as a
prelude to a solemn one last?
A. The temporary profession which is to be a prelude to a solemn or a simple perpetual profession, as a general rule, must be made for three years (can. 574, 1).

Some constitutions ordain that a profession be made year by year. This is indeed allowable and to be followed, when so ordained. However, the canonical rule still stands that no one is to be admitted to a perpetual profession unless three years of temporary vows have preceded.

If after three years from his first profession a religious will not have completed the required age of a perpetual profession, he may from the very start make a first profession of any length sufficient to cover the time to reach the required age of twenty-one years (can. 574, 1).

Q. 277. Can the three-year period of temporary profession
that is to precede a perpetual profession be extended?
A. It can be extended, but never beyond another three-year period (can. 574, 2). This second three-year period must be started immediately upon the expiration of the first (can. 577, 1), by renewing the profession.

Q. 278. What are the effects of a temporary profession?
A. The religious professed of only temporary vows:

1. Enjoy the same indulgences, privileges, and spiritual vows as the perpetually professed; and in case of death they are entitled to the same suffrages (can. 578, 1).

2. They have the obligation of observing the rule and constitutions just as the perpetually professed. However, they are not obliged, even in the institutes wherein the choral recitation of the Divine Office is imposed, to the private recitation of the Office, unless the constitutions expressly so ordain (can. 758, 2).

Q. 279. Is there an obligation to renew the temporary profession?

A. Upon the expiration of the time of the temporary vows, there is an obligation to renew the vows without delay; otherwise, one must leave the institute. A professed of temporary vows cannot remain without vows even for a day (can. 577, 1).

It is to be noted:

1. That the years in question are to be computed according to the calendar, following the norm of canon 34, 3, 1. Thus, if a religious made his temporary profession on March 1st for one year, the year is completed on March 1st of the following year, even if it is a leap year.

2. That the profession can be and must be renewed on the very same day in which the year or years of the vows will expire without need of waiting for the following day, and at any hour of that day (can. 34, 3, 5). For example, if a religious made his profession for one year on March 1, 1952, he may renew his profession on March 1, 1953 at any hour of that day, even if his profession in 1952 had been made at the last hour of the day.

Q. 280. Can the renewal of the profession be made before the time fixed for it?

A. Superiors have the faculty to permit, for sound reasons, the renewal of a profession before its fixed term, but only within one month of its fixed term (can. 577, 2).

However, the three-year, five-year, or six-year period that should precede the solemn or simple perpetual profession, even in the case of anticipating the renewal of a temporary profession, cannot be abbreviated. The perpetual profession, simple or solemn, can be made only when the three-year, five-year, or six-year period is completed.

Q. *281.* Upon the expiration of the time of temporary profession may one leave the institute?

A. Upon the expiration of the time of temporary profession a religious is fully free to leave the institute. Indeed, if he does not intend to renew the vows immediately, he is obliged to leave (can. 575, 1).

Q. *282.* Is the institute free upon the expiration of the vows to dismiss the religious?

A. Certainly! As long as the reasons are just, truly applicable in the case, and not only because of the state of health, unless it is a question of an illness maliciously concealed before the profession, the institute may dismiss the individual (can. 637).

Q. *283.* How is the profession to be renewed?

A. In order to have its legal effects continue the profession is always to be renewed publicly, that is, before the community or at least before the legitimate superiors, according to the norms of the constitutions. There is no obligation to have any external solemnity.

Therefore, the private renewal of the vows on the occasion of a great feast or in other circumstances, while being most commendable as an act of devotion and in confirmation of one's good will before God, canonically adds nothing in time or obligation to the profession publicly pronounced according to the form prescribed by the Church. Without juridical effects, these private renewals of vows are most beautiful acts of devotion on the part of religious, particularly when done during Holy Mass or reception of Holy Communion. Recently, the Church has granted to this practice an indulgence of three years (The Sacred Penitentiary, April 10, 1937).

Q. 284. Is the canonical examination required before a renewal of temporary profession?

A. It is not required. The Code prescribes the canonical examination only for admission to the novitiate, for first temporary profession, and for a perpetual profession (can. 552, 1). There is no mention of a canonical examination before renewing temporary vows.

Q. 285. Are witnesses required?

A. This is determined by the constitutions of each institute.

Q. 286. Are spiritual exercises required?

A. They are not required by the Code for the renewal of a temporary profession. The usage, however, of a short spiritual retreat before each renewal is commendable as we have said, Q. 240.

Q. 287. Must the renewal of profession be registered?

A. Certainly, just as the first profession, and the record is to be kept in the archives of the religious house (Q. 251).

Chapter 18

The Perpetual Profession

Q. *288.* When is a religious profession said to be perpetual?
A. A profession is perpetual when one takes the vows for the rest of his life (Q. 123).

Q. *289.* Is a perpetual profession simple or solemn?
A. It can be either. A solemn profession is always perpetual, while a simple one can be temporary or perpetual (Q. 263).

Q. *290.* What conditions are required for it to be valid?
A. A perpetual profession, simple or solemn, is not valid if:

1. The religious has not completed twenty-one years of age (can. 573; Q. 242).

2. If there has not preceded a simple temporary profession of at least three years (can. 572, 2).

With respect to these conditions, let it be noted:

1. That the three-year term of simple profession which necessarily must precede the perpetual profession has to be entire, ending on the same day of the same month in which it began. Thus if it began on March 1, 1952, it ends on March 1, 1955, without need of worrying about the hour of the day in which the three-year term ends (can. 34, 3, 5).

2. That this three-year term can be extended, either because

the religious has not as yet reached his twenty-first year of age required for a perpetual profession or by the will of the superiors, who, however, cannot extend it beyond another three-year term (can. 574, 1 and 2).

As we said in the note to Q. 276, if the required age will not be attained after three years from his first profession, he could make his first profession for the full period that will complete his twenty-one years. But if he will attain his majority before the expiration of the first three-year term, he must make his profession for a full three-year term, and any extension of it must come after the completion of this three-year term (can. 574, 2).

Q. 291. Is a canonical examination necessary before perpetual profession?

A. It is necessary for nuns and sisters according to the prescriptions of canon 522, 1. It is to be made at the time and in the mode cited for admission to the novitiate in Q. 86.

Q. 292. Is there an obligation to make perpetual profession?
A. If the constitutions prescribe only temporary vows, there is no obligation and there is no need to make a perpetual profession. If the constitutions permit the religious to make perpetual vows, then, the legal time having elapsed for the temporary profession, the religious, according to the Code, may pronounce perpetual vows, simple or solemn according to the constitutions of his institute, or else return to the world (can. 575, 1).

In institutes wherein perpetual vows are taken, it is not lawful to extend temporary vows at the pleasure of the religious or of the superiors. After the completion of six years at the most from one's first profession, one must either make perpetual profession or else return to the world.

Q. 293. What legal effects does a perpetual profession produce?

A. First, the religious professed of perpetual vows contracts all the obligations inherent in these vows according as they are simple or solemn (Qq. 155, 156, 188, 189, 207, 208). Secondly, whether he be in solemn or simple perpetual vows, he becomes an *apostate* if he leaves his religious house unlawfully with the intention not to return, or even if he has left lawfully, but does not return, willfully intending thereby to remove himself from the religious obedience due to his superiors (can. 644, 1).

Chapter 19

The Religious Habit

Q. *294.* Is there an obligation always to wear the religious habit of one's own institute?

A. Yes. Besides the constitutions of each religious institute, there is the law of the Church which prescribes that professed religious, "unless a weighty reason excuses them, must wear the habit of their institute both inside and outside their house" (can. 596).

Q. *295.* What can be considered a weighty reason to excuse them from wearing the habit?

A. A weighty reason would be the prohibition of its wearing by civil law, the custom of a people who resent it, and special circumstances of a social revolution, of a persecution, and so on. In these and similar circumstances, it is lawful to put aside or to conceal the religious habit.

The judgment as to the gravity of the case is not left to the individual religious, but "to the major superiors, and, in urgent cases, to the local superior" (can. 506).

Q. *296.* Are the novices obliged to wear the religious habit?

A. Yes, even the novices, "unless special circumstances of the place counsel otherwise, are obliged to wear the habit prescribed for them by the constitutions" (can. 557).

It is not obligatory that the novices wear a habit different from that of the professed, but they may have a different one. Whatever habit is prescribed by their constitutions must be worn during the time of their novitiate. Unless a grave reason prevents it, they should always wear a religious habit.

Q. 297. What is the obligation of postulants with reference to a habit?

A. Postulants should "dress modestly" (can. 540, 2). It is not necessary that they have a special religious dress. They may well continue to wear the same clothes they had in the world, as long as they are modest. If it be desired to give them a dress more or less religious "it must be different from that of the novices" (can. 540, 2).

Q. 298. What must be the nature of a religious habit?

A. Besides aiming at modesty, the religious garb must always be in accord with poverty. All that which smacks of superfluous finery or luxury must be avoided (*Motu Proprio,* St. Pius X, July 15, 1906).

Neither is it fitting for religious persons to carry gold or even silver articles, unless they be of common usage, such as a watch, a small cross, and the like.

Q. 299. Is a ring of gold or silver permitted?

A. It is permitted if it is so prescribed or allowed by the constitutions. However, it must never be a precious one, nor adorned with pearls, gems, diamonds, and such.

Q. 300. When is there the obligation to put aside the religious habit?

A. Even if they had been invested lawfully with the religious habit, the following are obliged to put it aside:

1. all those who have obtained from the Holy See the so-called indult of exclaustration (can. 639);

2. for a greater reason, all those who have obtained from the Holy See the so-called indult of secularization (can. 640, I, 1);

3. all those who have been expelled (can. 648; 649, 2);

4. all those who, having completed their term of temporary vows, leave the institute (can. 492, 3).

Q. 301. In order to obey the above cited laws concerning the laying aside of the religious habit, is it enough to conceal it instead of laying it aside?

A. No, it is not enough if we are to follow the tenor of canons 639 and 640, which clearly impose the obligation of putting aside the habit, at least in its external appearance. Putting aside a thing is not the same as hiding it.

It is not forbidden, however, to wear some of the underclothing that was prescribed in that institute, nor is it wrong to wear the small habit, called the scapular, which is used by the tertiaries of some religious orders. At all events, one must not wear the religious habit any longer, at least in its external appearance.

Chapter 20

~~~~~~~~~~

The Cloister

~~~~~~~~~~

Q. 302. What is meant by the cloister?
A. Materially speaking the cloister is the place wherein religious dwell so as to perform more freely their duties to God. Formally speaking a cloister is an obligation not to enter a convent or a part of it, or to leave it without lawful permission.

Q. 303. How many kinds of cloisters are there?
A. Two, papal and episcopal. A papal cloister is prescribed for nuns and male religious with solemn vows. An episcopal cloister is the one prescribed either by common law or by a bishop for male religious or for sisters with simple vows.

A papal cloister for religious women of solemn vows recently has been reorganized to include a major and a minor cloister. The major cloister imposes on the nuns the strict obligation never to leave its precincts without apostolic dispensation. The minor cloister allows one or another religious, for the time necessary to attend to some apostolic work, to go beyond the portion of the monastery strictly reserved to the nuns without need of an apostolic dispensation, for example to conduct school, to teach catechism, and so on. They may leave to go to the part of the monastery designated for such apostolic work, and when there is real need for the apostolic work they may even go beyond the precincts of the monastery itself.[18]

Q. 304. What kind of cloister is to be observed by male religious?

A. Religious who are regulars, that is, male religious with solemn vows, are obliged, even in their nonformed houses, to observe a papal cloister (can. 597). Religious men with simple vows, such as members of a religious congregation, have a cloister which is not papal but episcopal (can. 2342).

Q. 305. What kind of cloister must religious women keep?

A. In the canonically erected monasteries of nuns, even if they are not formed, if no extraneous apostolic work has been indicated to them, the papal cloister has to be observed (can. 597, 1).

If external apostolic work has been assigned to them, then they observe the law of the minor papal cloister conformable with their particular constitutions legitimately approved.

Even in the houses of sisters, whether their institute be of papal or of diocesan law, a cloister has to be observed, an episcopal one in their case. The mode of its observance varies with the constitutions of each institute.

Q. 306. Who are obliged to observe the law of the cloister in the convents of regulars?

A. In the convents of regulars who are men with solemn vows, the cloister restrains only women of whatever age or condition from entering. A lone exception is the wife of the chief executive or ruler of a state, together with her retinue (can. 598, 2).

Q. 307. Who are obliged to the law of the cloister in monasteries of nuns?

A. Since we must now distinguish between a major and a minor cloister due to the Constitution *Sponsa Christi* of No-

18 Constitution, *Sponsa Christi*, November 21, 1950.

vember 21, 1950, which was followed on November 23, 1950, by Instructions of the Sacred Congregation of Religious, the laws of the major cloister in the monasteries of nuns concern:

1. The nuns themselves, for they are severely prohibited, after their profession, under pain of excommunication, from leaving the precincts of the monastery, even for a short time and for whatever reason, without a special indult of the Holy See, unless of course there is danger of death or of some other grievous calamity (can. 2342, 1).

"After the profession" means that the postulants and novices are excluded from this regulation. Religious women who have been admitted to postulancy or novitiate do not need any special permission if they intend to quit the institute, but once they do leave the monastery, they can never return to it (Q. 103).

2. Outsiders, no matter what their rank or category, of either sex, of any age or condition, for all these are forbidden under penalty of excommunication to enter the precincts of the cloister in the monastery of nuns without special and proper permission (can. 600; 2342, 1).

Excepted from this prohibition are the following persons:

1. The ordinary of the place and the regular superior, together with visitors sent by them or delegated by the Holy See. All these may enter the precincts of the cloister, not at their own pleasure, but only for reason of inspection, and in so doing, they must be accompanied by another cleric or religious of mature age (can. 600, 1).

"For reason of inspection" means that even in times of visitation it is not lawful to enter the cloister to interrogate the nuns, which can and should be done at the grille. The entry into the cloister is permissible only when a nun is sick or otherwise incapable of going to the grille for the interrogation.

2. The confessor, or his substitute. These, taking due precaution, may enter the cloister so as to administer the sacraments to the sick and to assist the dying (can. 600, 2).

The confessor here means the ordinary one, the extraordinary one, and anyone else deputed, including any priest approved for the confessions of women who is requested by a nun gravely ill to hear her confession. If it is a case of imminent danger of death, any priest may hear the confession of a dying nun (Qq. 327 ff.).

By the phrase, "or his substitute," is meant the priest who ordinarily administers the sacraments of the Eucharist and extreme unction, for example, the chaplain. When Holy Communion is desired to be received out of devotion, any priest who celebrates Mass for the nuns, or who is called by them, may in the place of the confessor or the chaplain, enter the cloister to administer Holy Communion to the sick.

"Taking due precaution" means the following:

1. In the administration of Holy Communion, four sisters, of mature age if possible, must accompany the priest from the time of his entering to the time of his leaving the cloister (Sacred Congregation of Religious, February 6, 1924).

2. In the administration of the sacrament of penance, two nuns must accompany the confessor from his entrance into the cloister to the cell of the sick nun, and await him there at the door, which is to be kept open until he has finished hearing the confession, and then accompany him to the exit of the cloister. The same rule is to prevail for the administering of extreme unction, or for the last prayers, and so on, but in these cases the attendant nuns, as well as any other members of the community, may enter the cell of the sick religious. As soon as the confession or other priestly function, for which they have lawfully entered the cloister, is over, the priests must immediately leave the cloister.

3. The chief executives or rulers of the state, with their wives and retinue (can. 600, 3).

"The chief executives or rulers of the state" means not only the emperor, the king, or reigning prince, but also the president of a republic and all those who are commonly recognized as and are the chief executives of a state, no matter what they may be called. Excluded are cabinet members, prefects, members of the legislature, magistrates, and the like.[19]

"With their wives" means the lawful consorts of these chief executives of a state. Should the head of a state be a woman, her lawful husband would be allowed to accompany her into a cloister.

"Retinue" means the entire group which the chief executive has invited to accompany him and which forms his cortege.

4. The cardinals of the Holy Roman Church, with their retinue (can. 600, 3).

5. Physicians, surgeons, and whoever may be necessary for the needs of the monastery (can. 600, 3). For all these, however, the permission of the ordinary of the place must be sought, a standing permission sufficing. If the need is urgent, with no time to seek the permission, it can properly be presumed. However, the due precautions must always be taken.

The laws of the minor cloister prescribe:

1. That a definite portion of the monastery be reserved exclusively for the nuns while another portion be set aside for apostolic activities.

2. It is absolutely forbidden, under penalty of excommunication reserved to the Holy See, to allow any outside person of either sex, or of any age and condition to enter the portion reserved for the nuns, except those persons enumerated above in reference to the major cloister.

3. It is equally forbidden to nuns after their profession to go out of the monastery, as was said concerning the nuns of major papal enclosure. It is permitted them to leave the cloister only for the place reserved for the apostolic works according to the norm of the constitution cited above, and only for the reason of attending to the work. For this reason, and only when it is necessary, which judgment rests gravely on the conscience of both the superior and the ordinary, nuns who are

[19] *Translator's note:* In the United States, the president would enjoy this privilege, as would also the governors of each of the States. In Canada, the governor general is included in the privilege.

expert in certain apostolic work may even go outside the monastery.

4. In the places reserved for the apostolic work, only the pupils, boys or girls, or those for whom the work is done, including any women who in view of the work to be done have reason to be admitted, may enter. For males to enter, other than the boy pupils, there is required the permission of the ordinary.

5. Nuns who unlawfully leave the part of the monastery exclusively reserved for them to go to the places reserved for the apostolic works should be severely punished by their superior or by the ordinary. Likewise, those who unlawfully allow unauthorized persons to enter the places reserved for the apostolic works should be severely punished.

Q. 308. May nuns, even those enclosed by a major cloister, use a terrace or the roof of their monastery for a walk or airing?

A. They may, provided the terrace is protected by a grille all around so that the nuns cannot be seen.[20]

Q. 309. In monasteries with either a major or minor cloister, may nuns, at least some of them, go into that part of the church reserved for the faithful to set up things needed for services, to clean, and so forth, in those hours when the faithful are not present?

A. They may not do so without special permission. In view of the need there is for this sort of work in the church, the Holy See, when requested, is accustomed to grant to the superior the power to designate some nuns to go into the church when it is closed to the faithful to clean and to prepare things needed in the sacred functions.[21]

Q. 310. To whom is entrusted the custodianship of the cloister in monasteries of nuns?

[20] Instructions of the Sacred Congregation of Religious, February 6, 1924.
[21] *Ibid.*

A. The cloister in a monastery of nuns, even if the monastery is subject to the regular superior, is entrusted principally to the vigilance of the ordinary of the place. He can reprove and punish any transgressor, even an exempt regular, with penalties including censure (can. 603, 1).

The regular superior, in the monasteries subject to him, also has the responsibility of guarding the cloister, and he can punish the transgressors if they are under his jurisdiction, be they nuns or others (can. 603, 2).

Q. 311. What precautions are to be taken when an outside person is to be admitted into the cloister reserved for the nuns with due permission?

A. The precautions to be taken in these cases are indicated in a document of the Sacred Congregation of Religious issued February 16, 1924, namely:

1. that reliable information be previously secured concerning the person to be admitted into the cloister and that he be found to be of the best reputation and of unimpeachable character;

2. he is to be accompanied always by two nuns of mature bearing;

3. no other nun is permitted to talk to this outside person except for the reason for which he was admitted into the cloister.

Q. 312. What canonical penalties does one incur if he violates the cloister of religious men?

A. All women who violate the cloister of regulars, and any other person, including the superiors whoever they are, who have brought in and admitted any woman of whatever age, are *ipso facto* excommunicated, the excommunication being simply reserved to the Holy See (can. 2342, 2).

Q. 313. What penalties are incurred by those who violate the cloister of nuns?

A. Whoever, of whatever degree, rank or sex, violates the

major cloister of nuns, either by entering without lawful permission or by bringing in and admitting within the confines of the major cloister any person who does not belong there, immediately incurs excommunication reserved simply to the Holy See (can. 2342, 1). The same is to be said for the minor cloister, since that part of the monastery is reserved exclusively for the nuns.

Also immediately excommunicated are the nuns who after their profession unlawfully leave the confines of the major cloister or of the minor cloister if their cloister is minor. This excommunication is also reserved simply to the Holy See (can. 2342, 3).

Q. 314. What penalties are incurred by those who violate the cloister in convents and in monasteries of religious congregations?
A. The bishop may in special circumstances and for grave reasons safeguard the cloister in convents and monasteries of religious congregations of men or women by imposing censures (can. 604, 3).

However, these censures can never be of the canonical kind or those imposed by the common law of the Church on those who violate a papal cloister, since the cloister in a convent or monastery of a congregation is not a papal one.

Q. 315. For what period of time may religious men or women remain outside their convent with only the permission of their superiors?
A. Superiors, whoever they are, cannot permit their men or women religious who are subject to them to remain outside of the convent for more than six months. For a longer period, permission must be sought from the pope (can. 606).

The only exception is the case of sending a religious outside the convent for the sake of studies, provided that the usual precautions are taken.

Chapter 21

The Confessors

Q. *316.* To whom may religious men go for confession?

A. For nonexempt religious clerical institutions and for exempt lay religious institutes the rule is that their members may go for confession only to those confessors approved for all the faithful by the ordinary of the place, or to those who as ordinary or extraordinary confessors have been appointed by the bishop for a specific religious house.

The members of exempt clerical institutes may licitly and validly always have their confessions heard either by confessors approved for all the faithful by the ordinary of the place, or by confessors who have been designated by the religious superior as confessors for their own religious according to the norm of the constitutions (can. 519, 875).

Q. *317.* How many kinds of confessors are there with reference to religious women?

A. According to the law presently prevailing, we may distinguish five kinds of confessors with reference to religious women, namely, the ordinary, the extraordinary, the supplementary, the occasional, and the special.

The ordinary are the confessors lawfully deputized to hear habitually the confessions of the members of an entire community of religious women (can. 520, 1).

The extraordinary are those confessors lawfully appointed to hear the confessions of an entire community of religious women at least four times a year, which is generally done during the ember weeks (can. 521, 1).

The supplementary are those confessors who in addition to the ordinary and the extraordinary are declared by the bishop as approved to hear the confessions of religious women of one or more communities whenever, in particular cases, they may be called for that service (can. 521, 2).

The occasional are all those confessors approved for women in general who in exceptional circumstances can validly and licitly hear the confession of religious women. For this reason they are called occasional (can. 530, 2; 523).

The special are those confessors who, for special reasons, are sent by the bishop, even habitually, as a concession to one or another religious woman for the quieting of her conscience and for greater advancement in the life of perfection (can. 520, 2).

Q. 318. What is the difference among ordinary, extraordinary, and supplementary confessors?

A. The difference between the ordinary confessor and the extraordinary one lies in the fact that the ordinary confessor is deputed to hear *habitually* the confessions of religious women, that is, whenever the rule prescribes the confessions or whenever the religious women may request confession. These religious women may not go elsewhere unless there is a definite reason. The extraordinary confessor is delegated to hear the confessions of the religious women only at certain times of the year, which, according to the Code are not to be less than four times.

The supplementary confessors differ from the ordinary and the extraordinary in this: that while the supplementary confessor may hear, even habitually, one or several religious women who for good reasons desire him, and while he may in particular cases hear even the entire community, as we will

further explain in Question 326, there never exists the obligation on the part of the religious women to approach him.

The occasional, as we said above, can hear the confession
of only one or two religious women in special and occasional
circumstances. We shall have more to say about him later.

The special confessor is authorized to hear the confession
not of the community but of only one or two of the religious
women not only occasionally but even habitually.

Q. *319.* Who has the power to approve the confessors of religious women?
A. The power to approve confessors of religious women is
vested always in the bishop of the place in which the religious
house is located (can. 876, 1, 2). These exceptions, however, are
to be noted:

1. If the religious house is immediately subject to the Holy
See or to their own ordinary, all the confessors are to be appointed and approved by them (can. 525).

2. If the religious house is subject to the regular superior,
this superior will present to the ordinary the names of all the
confessors to be approved. Only when the regular superior
shows any negligence in presenting these names can the ordinary go ahead and name the needed confessors (can. 525).

Q. *320.* How long may the ordinary confessor remain in office?
A. The ordinary confessor can be approved only for a three-
year period (can. 526). He cannot be approved for another
three-year period for the same community until one year has
elapsed from the time he ended his first three-year term (can.
524, 2). However, if the bishop finds it difficult to provide
priests qualified for the office, or if the major number of the
religious women of the community, including those who for
other matters have not the right to give their vote, evidences
by secret vote a desire to retain the ordinary confessor, for

either of these reasons he may reappoint the confessor for another three-year term immediately, without waiting for the prescribed one-year interval. For the same reasons he may proceed to appoint him for a third three-year term (can. 576). Should some of the religious women have shown themselves opposed to the confirmation, the bishop shall have to provide for them a second confessor in addition to the one confirmed (can. 526).

For an ordinary confessor to be appointed beyond a third three-year term without an intervening period the bishop must have recourse to the pope.

Q. 321. May an ordinary confessor whose three-year term has expired in one community be named as ordinary confessor for another community without the need of the intervening period?

A. Yes, he may be appointed immediately.

Q. 322. May there be more than one ordinary confessor for a community?

A. Usually there should be only one ordinary confessor for each community. However, for communities which are large or when any other just cause suggests it, two or more ordinary confessors may be appointed (can. 520, 1).

Q. 323. Is there an obligation on the part of the religious women to make use of the extraordinary confessor?

A. They have the obligation to go to him at least to receive his blessing (can. 521, 1).

Q. 324. Why is it said that they must go to him "at least to receive his blessing"?

A. If the religious woman does not deem it helpful to her conscience to approach the extraordinary confessor for confession, she has only the obligation of approaching him in the confessional to ask for his blessing.

The reason for this prudent provision is obvious. Were some of the religious women to approach the extraordinary confessor while some others did not, the suspicion would easily arise that some of the religious women had need of the extraordinary confessor while others did not. All this would place in jeopardy one's liberty of conscience. To prevent any embarrassment, the Church prudently prescribes that all and each of the religious, without exception, must present themselves to the extraordinary confessor. If they want to make their confession to him, well and good. If not, they simply ask for his blessing, and no one will know for what reason the religious woman went into the confessional.

Q. 325. Are the extraordinary confessors subject to the rule of the three-year term?
A. They are not subject to it (The Sacred Congregation of Religious, December 7, 1906).

Q. 326. When may the supplementary confessors be called by religious women?
A. Only in special cases (can. 521, 2).

Q. 327. What is meant by "special cases"?
A. We mean when it is a question of hearing the confession of one or two religious women and there is present some definite need or at least some spiritual usefulness. A definite need, for example, could be the absence of the ordinary confessor, in which case the supplementary could hear the confessions of individual religious women and even of the entire community.

Q. 328. If a religious woman, for the quieting of her conscience, demands a special confessor, must the ordinary concede him to her?
A. The Code does not oblige him, saying only that in these cases the ordinary should be easily disposed to concede the request. He must be vigilant always to prevent abuses. Should

they arise, he must carefully and prudently correct them. However, he must preserve the religious woman's liberty of conscience (can. 520, 2). For this reason the Church provides for the special confessor.

Q. 329. If a religious woman is gravely ill, may she call for a confessor who is not the ordinary, the extraordinary, or the supplementary?
A. Yes, for canon 523 reads: "If a religious woman, whoever she is, is gravely ill, even though she is not in danger of death, she may call for any priest approved for the hearing of women's confessions, and confess to him as often as she wishes during the period of her illness, nor may her superior in any way, directly or indirectly, forbid it." The confessor in this case is an occasional one.

Q. 330. May a religious woman outside the case of grave illness, for the peace of her conscience, ask for any confessor approved for the confession of women?
A. She may ask for him but the confession is to be made in a church or oratory, even a semi-public one (can. 522), or in any place lawfully approved for the confession of women (Pontifical Commission for the Interpretation of the Code, February 26, 1920). In this case as well the priest is an occasional confessor.

Q. 331. What does the phrase "for the peace of her conscience" mean?
A. It means that there must be present the motive of spiritual utility. It is up to the confessor to judge whether or not this proper motive is present.

Q. 332. If a religious woman asks for a confessor who is the extraordinary, or supplementary, or occasional, is it lawful for her superior to investigate directly or indirectly, by herself or by means of another, the reason for such a request?

A. She may not do so; neither may she deny in any way the request for the desired confessor, or appear in any way displeased (can. 521, 3).

Q. 333. Is the superior of a house where there is no cloister obliged to grant to her subjects the requested permission to leave the house each time they desire to go to confession?

A. No. The Code, canon 522, as above cited, while granting to religious women the right to have their confessions heard in the church or in any oratory by any confessor approved for women, which privileges they may validly and licitly use, does not wish the religious women to assume any right to withdraw themselves for that reason from the regular discipline or from the obedience due to their superiors. If the sister happens to find herself out of the house for any reason she may take advantage of it by going to the parish church and having her confession heard there without need of securing permission either from the bishop or from her superior. However, she may not demand from her superior permission to leave the house for the sole purpose of having her confession heard in the parish church. The superior may very well deny the permission in this case.

Q. 334. Is it permissible for the superior to demand that her subjects reveal to her matters of conscience?

A. It is not permissible (can. 530, 1).

Therefore, even if the rules prescribe a so-called weekly or monthly conference with the superior, this is to be understood as referring only to external matters, such as occupation, work, corporal health, and the like. Concerning internal matters of conscience, neither the rule nor the superior can demand any revelation in any way, as long as the religious woman does not wish to do so of her own accord.

Of course, should the religious woman freely and of her own accord wish to open her mind before her superior, she may do so. It is good to show a filial confidence in one's superior (can. 530, 1).

Chapter 22

The Divine Office

Q. *335.* What is meant by the Divine Office?

A. By Divine Office is meant that series of vocal and public prayers ordered by the Church to be recited daily by certain designated persons in the name of the Church.

These prayers are also called the canonical hours, because they are to be recited in certain determined hours of the day as the liturgical laws of the Church prescribe. They are also called the breviary, since the prayers of the Divine Office are nothing more than a brief compendium of the Old and New Testaments, of the homilies of the Fathers, and of the lives of many of the saints.

Q. *336.* How many parts are there in the Divine Office?

A. There are seven parts, namely, Matins and Lauds, which count as one; 2, Prime; 3, Tierce; 4, Sext; 5, None; 6, Vespers, and 7, Compline.

This septenary division is drawn from verse 164 of Psalm 118, wherein the Psalmist exclaims: "Seven times a day I have given praise to Thee for the judgments of Thy justice."

Matins is divided into three parts, called nocturns, for the reason that in ancient times these parts were recited at night separately from the others in the three vigils or awaitings in the night. Lauds is recited in the fourth vigil, towards the dawning, and hence is considered joined to the nocturns, thus forming with them the Matins, one of the seven parts of the Divine Office. The word Matins was introduced into the liturgy when the separate recitation of the nocturnal vigils was no longer demanded, but only of the nocturns together, with Lauds as the fourth vigil. This last of the vigils ended at dawn, hence it was called the *ante-lucanum,* which means, before the light or morning vigil.

Matins with Lauds as one hour and Vespers as another are called the major canonical hours, while the others are minor canonical hours.

Q. 337. When was the recitation of the Divine Office or of the so-called canonical hours introduced in the Church?
A.   As far as the substance of the prayer is concerned, we can say that it goes back to the time of the apostles. We read in the Acts of the Apostles that they went to the Temple daily at certain hours to pray. Thus we read: "Now Peter and John went up into the temple at the ninth hour of prayer" (Acts, 3, 1).

As to the form, it gradually evolved and perfected itself in the course of the centuries. The present actual form of the breviary comes to us from the Middle Ages. It was modified and perfected under the pontificates of St. Pius V, of Clement VIII, and of Urban VIII. The latest reform, particularly in reference to the recitation of the Psalms, was introduced during the reign of St. Pius X.

Q. 338. Who are obliged under grave penalty, that is, under pain of mortal sin, to recite daily the Divine Office?
A.   The following are so obliged:
    1. Clerics in major orders, that is, all those who have been ordained subdeacons (can. 139).
    2. Canons and those possessing a benefice (can. 1175).
    3. Religious clerics who are solemnly professed (can. 610, 3).

Q. 339. Are religious women ever obliged under mortal sin to recite the Office?

A. Generally speaking, nuns who have taken solemn vows and are assigned to choral duties are obliged under grave penalty (can. 610, 3). All others, who have simple vows, if any obligation is imposed, have it merely as a constitutional obligation.

Q. 340. When does this obligation begin for those men and women religious who must recite the Office under grave penalty?

A. It begins from the moment of their solemn profession, the one professed being obliged to begin with that hour of the Divine Office which corresponds to that hour of the day in which he has been professed. Thus, if one were professed in the morning after 6 but before 9 o'clock, he should begin with Tierce; before noon, with Sext; before 3 P.M., with None; before 6 P.M., with Vespers, and before 9 in the evening, with Compline.

Q. 341. What breviary and ordo must religious men and women use for the recitation of their Office?

A. They must use the breviary and the ordo or calendar approved for each order (Sacred Congregation of Religious, February 28, 1914).

If they have no ordo of their own they must use that of the diocese in which they are located. While traveling, for the private recitation of their Office, religious must use the ordo of the religious house to which they are assigned. If they find themselves in another religious house and go to choir there, they may, and even should, follow the ordo of that house (Sacred Congregation of Religious, September 25, 1852; June 27, 1896).

Q. 342. In how many ways can the Office be recited?

A. It can be recited publicly, that is in choir, one side alternating with the other, and it can be recited privately, that is, out of choir, each individual attending privately to his recitation of it.

Q. *343.* When is it obligatory for religious to recite the Office publicly, that is, in choir?

A. In those religious communities which are obliged to the choral recitation of the Office, the obligation to do it chorally is always present when there are at least four religious bound to the Office in the house and not legitimately impeded from going to choir (can. 610, 1). This obligation can be binding even if there are less than four, should the particular constitutions so prescribe.

Q. *344.* How many religious are required to satisfy the choral obligation?

A. Four of them certainly suffice. Probably, three suffice, and even two, since the Code says that the particular constitutions can oblige the religious to the choral recitation even if less than four are available. Hence two religious can constitute a choir.

Q. *345.* Can the laybrothers or laysisters, the novices and religious who have made only simple profession be counted for the number necessary to constitute a choir?

A. Laybrothers and laysisters cannot be counted for this (The Sacred Congregation of Bishops and Regulars, August 6, 1858).

Clerics and choir religious women with simple vows, however, can be counted.

With reference to novices, male or female, the Church has not given a definite ruling, while writers on religious observance are not yet in agreement to include or exclude them. At all events, that they may be counted seems to be the most probable opinion, for if we employ the rule of *"In favorabilibus,"* namely, "In favorable things privileges are to be amplified," *novices* can be classed as religious, and so can be counted for choir.

Q. 346. In what time is it permitted to satisfy the obligation?

A. If it is a question of a public recitation, that is, in choir, the present-day liturgy ordains:

Matins and Lauds are to be recited from midnight to noon. Their recitation can even be anticipated on the day before from the moment on that preceding day when the sun is nearer its setting than it is to its zenith, which can be reckoned as about three hours before its setting.

Prime, Tierce, Sext are to be recited before noon, while None may be recited either before noon or after noon.

Vespers and Compline are to be recited after noon and before midnight. In Lent, Vespers on weekdays should be recited before noon.

In the case of private recitation, that is, outside of choir, then for pure validity it suffices to recite the Office from one midnight to the other. For it to be licit, the liturgy prescribes that the Office be said in correspondence of its hours with the periods of the day as cited above, unless a just reason prevents it. Further, it is granted that Matins may be anticipated from 2 P.M. of the preceding day (Sacred Congregation of Rites, May 12, 1905).

Q. 347. Would it be a sin not to recite the Divine Office in the periods of the day enumerated above?

A. If it is done without any reason, it is certainly a sin, at least a venial one, for the laws of the liturgy oblige one in conscience. However, particularly in the private recitation, any reasonable cause would justify its recitation at any hour of the day without incurring sin.

Q. 348. Where is the Divine Office to be recited?

A. The public recitation of the Divine Office should be made in church, and particularly in that part of the church reserved to clerics and called the choir. For any good reason, for instance, the coldness of the church, or while repairs are being made, the Office can be said in a chapel or in any smaller choir or alcove attached to the church (Sacred Congregation of Rites, December 12, 1879).

For the private recitation the Office can be recited in any decent place free of distractions, at least of deliberate ones.

Q.   349. In what order should the Divine Office be recited?
A.   There are two considerations with reference to the order in which the Divine Office must be recited: first, the kind or title of the total Office, and secondly, the order of its hours.

As to the kind or title, that particular Office which is indicated in the ordo or calendar for that day is to be recited, be it festive or ferial.

As to the order of the hours, it must be recited in the order in which the breviary sets the succession of the hours, namely, Matins and Lauds, Prime, Tierce, Sext, None, Vespers, and Compline.

Q.   350. Does *Pretiosa* form part of the Office, and if it does, at which point must it be recited?
A.   *Pretiosa* does form an integral part of the Office, and it is to be recited immediately after Lauds if that hour with its Matins has been recited in the morning; but if Matins and Lauds have been anticipated the evening before, it is to be said immediately after Prime.

Under the name of *Pretiosa* are those prayers which customarily are recited in choir after the martyrology and which begin with the words: *Pretiosa in conspectu Domini mors sanctorum ejus*—Precious in the sight of the Lord is the death of His saints.

Q.   351. Is there an obligation to follow the order above described?
A.   Yes. Unless there is a good reason to excuse it, any deliberate disruption of the order is in sin, at least a venial one.

Q. 352. What would be some of the just reasons for changing the order of the hours?

A. Some of the reasons would be the following:

1. If a religious comes into choir finding that the Office has already begun. In this case he can join with the choir, and later make up the hours, or hour or part of it missed.

2. If a religious is invited to join another or others in the private recitation of the Office and it is found that one of them has already recited some of the hours, they should start reciting the Office at the point of the greatest advancement of any office-sayer in the group, the previous part of the Office to be said later.

3. If a religious finds himself with only a diurnal, he may start from there, and later add Matins and Lauds.

Q. 353. May each of the canonical hours be recited with intervals between them?

A. Certainly, for thus it was done in ancient times, as we said above, while it is still the practice in many monasteries of contemplative monks.

Q. 354. May there be an interval between Matins and Lauds?

A. In a private recitation, yes, and even if there is no particular reason. However, when this is done, at the end of the three nocturns, the Te Deum, if required that day, and the Pater Noster should be added. According to some authorities the recitation should end with the prayer of the day.

In the choral or public recitation, Matins may not be separated from Lauds without permission of the Holy See.

Q. 355. May the three nocturns of Matins be recited separately?

A. In a private recitation, yes, particularly if the interval does not exceed three hours which was the ancient spacing. But there should be a good reason. In choir or public recitation it may no longer be done.

Q. 356. May a psalm or an hour be interrupted?
A. Only if there is a good reason to do so. With a good reason it is permitted, as long as the interruption is not too long, for it would then break the moral union of the parts of the hour one with another.

Q. 357. What would be a good reason?
A. A good reason might be the need of doing immediately something which cannot be put off without inconvenience to oneself or to another, for example, the need of hearing the confession of one or two persons, of giving Holy Communion, and the like.

Other justifying reasons may be the obligation of urbanity, namely, to greet and converse with someone who has addressed the religious, and, of course, if one is given a command which requires immediate fulfillment.

Q. 358. Must he who recites the Office pronounce every word?
A. Certainly, because the Office is a vocal prayer.

Q. 359. Is it necessary that he hear himself?
A. That is not necessary. It is enough that the words be enunciated. The command is to recite the Office, not to hear it; wherefore, it suffices that one be aware he is pronouncing the words, even if by reason of some accompanying noise or other distraction he does not actually hear the words.

Q. 360. Besides the precise enunciation of the words, what else is demanded for the proper recitation of the Office?
A. That it be recited with intention and attention.

Q. 361. What is the intention?
A. In general the intention means the deliberate will to do or not to do a certain thing. In the present case it means the deliberate will to say the Office.

Q. 362. How many kinds of intention are there?

A. Intention can be actual, virtual, or implicit. It is actual when an act of the will effectively accompanies here and now the action it commands. It is virtual when, having been formed in the past as an actual intention to do a certain thing, that intention is never withdrawn, and hence applies now to the action. It is implicit when, although a certain action was not expressly mentioned in an intention of the will, the intention to perform that action was necessarily included in the nature of the actual intention made.

Q. 363. Which of these intentions must the religious have in order to satisfy his Office?

A. It is not required that he always have an actual intention. It is enough that it be virtual or implicit. He who contracts the obligation to recite the Office should, from the start of it at his profession, make the actual intention to pay and to discharge the obligation of the Office as the Church prescribes. It is praiseworthy of him frequently to renew this intention at the start of each day's Office, and of its parts, and even in the midst of its recitation. However, once the intention has been made at the beginning of the obligation or at the start of each day's Office, even if the religious no longer adverts to the intention, it suffices as long as it was never retracted. In the original intention made, the resolution is formed to keep saying the Office according to the mind of the Church without limitation of time. The same can be said for the implicit intention, since the action of one taking his breviary and going to choir is a manifest sign, even if he does not explicitly mention it, of his intention to fulfill his obligation.

Q. 364. What is meant by attention?

A. In general attention is the application of the mind to what is being done. In the present case it means that one should be constantly aware that he is reciting the Office.

Q. *365.* How many kinds of attention may there be?

A. Attention may be either internal or external. Internal attention is the awareness of the mind of what is being done; external attention consists in the avoiding of any external action detrimental to the internal attention or incompatible with the task being performed. For example, when one is reciting his Office he must avoid talking with anyone, writing, listening to anyone, and engaging in any other distracting activity.

Q. *366.* What attention is demanded for satisfying the obligation of the Office?

A. External attention is always required. Hence, if while reciting his Office one is voluntarily distracted by any action incompatible with the recitation of the Office, he does not satisfy his obligation.

Internal attention is also required, for the recitation of the Office cannot be reduced to a mere mechanical utterance of words. However, in the present case, what is called spiritual, literal, or even material internal attention will suffice.

Spiritual attention is had when one who is reciting the Office elevates his mind to God in contemplation of the divine mysteries of the life of our Lord, of His passion, of the divine attributes, and of other spiritual themes.

Literal attention is had when the reciter concentrates on the literal sense of the words that he utters.

Material attention is had when, while one does not understand or reflect on the sense of the words, he is concerned at least in carefully pronouncing the words.

Q. *367.* In practice, what is the best kind of attention?

A. The best kind of attention is spiritual attention by which we raise our mind to God, and concentrate on the divine mysteries. Literal attention suffices, as also does material attention, according to the consensus of all authorities.

Q. *368.* Do distractions invalidate the recitation of the Office?
A. As long as the distractions are involuntary, even if they continue unduly, they do not invalidate the Office. However, one must seek to banish them.

Q. *369.* What remedies can be employed to remove them?
A. The remedies can be either negative or positive. The negative remedies consist in avoiding all that which can be a source of distraction, such as noncustody of the eyes, talking, listening to conversations, and the like. The positive remedies consist in cultivating the presence of God, in making a sincere intention at the start of the Office, in the renewal of the intention, and in similar pious practices.

Q. *370.* May the Office be said while walking, while riding in a bus, a car, tram, train, and other conveyances?
A. Yes, provided that one avoids excessive distraction.

Q. *371.* May one recite the Office while in bed?
A. Rarely, except for some good reason, since there is danger of irreverence. A good reason might be excessive tiredness, or a physical condition making it inconvenient for one to stand or sit.

Q. *372.* If one through error or even through inadvertence says an Office different from the one assigned by the ordo for that day, does it satisfy his obligation?
A. Yes, it does. There is no need to say the one he should have said, for there is an ancient rule (*Officium pro officio valet*) that one Office is as good as another.

As soon as one becomes aware that he is saying the wrong Office, he should immediately change to the correct one, resuming it at the point of his advertence in conformity with another rule: *Error corrigitur ubi deprehenditur*—An error is corrected at the place it is detected.

Q. *373.* If one through inadvertence says the Office due for the following day, may he on the following day say the Office he missed on the preceding day?

A. No, he must recite the one appointed for that day, even though he had said that Office the day before. No one voluntarily may change the Office which the Church appoints for any particular day.

Q. *374.* Outside of choir, may several religious assemble to say the Office together?

A. Indeed they may, as long as they form two choirs and no more, so that the verses and the psalms are recited alternately as is done regularly in choir. If three or more persons recite the Office together, each one taking a verse in turn, they do not satisfy the obligation, for then it would not be alternating or in the form of a dialogue as the usage requires.

Q. *375.* If one cannot recite the Office by himself, is he obliged to seek a partner?

A. No, there is no strict obligation. Of course, should he seek a partner under the circumstances, it would be zealous and praiseworthy.

Q. *376.* Must this partner himself be obliged to the Office?
A. No, that is not necessary.

Q. *377.* If one, while attending choir, has had to absent himself for part of the recitation in order to perform certain duties encumbent upon him, such as ringing the bell, vesting, preparing the books, and so on, must he later make up for the part of the Office he has missed?

A. If it concerns only negligible parts, for example, some verses of a psalm, a response, an oration, and the like, there is no obligation to make them up. But if he has missed a notable part of the Office, particularly if it were an entire hour, he is obliged to recite it privately.

Q. 378. Are there reasons to excuse one from the recitation of the Office?

A. Yes, and they reduce themselves to three kinds: by reason of dispensation, by reason of charity, and by reason of impotence.

Q. 379. Who can dispense from the recitation of the Office?

A. 1. The pope for whatever reason he deems good.

2. The bishop, when an urgency exists, and then only in favor of a particular subject and for a short time. This is admitted by all, the right to do this stemming not from actual law but from legitimate custom.

3. If they are ordinaries in the sense of canon 198, the major superiors of exempt religious orders in favor of their own subjects and only in those cases in which the bishop can dispense.

Q. 380. May the local religious superiors dispense?

A. They may, by reason of an ancient and legitimate custom, in particular cases and for just cause, commute the entire Office or part of it and impose in its stead another good work. This is not to be regarded as a dispensation. They may, however, as superiors, declare with authority that there exists a sufficiently grave reason for the Office not to oblige in any particular case.

Q. 381. When does the dispensation by reason of charity exist?

A. When in the remaining time of the day for the saying of the Office there occurs the need to do something the omission of which would cause grave detriment to oneself or one's neighbor, a dispensation by reason of charity may be said to exist. The grave detriment must be real and the performance of the charitable act done to avoid the harm must truly be incompatible with the saying of the Office, at least morally so, as, for example, having to minister to the sick.

Q. 382. What is meant by impotence as a reason excusing one from the recitation of the Office?

A. We mean here a physical or moral impossibility of reciting the Office. It is physical when it is absolutely impossible to fulfill the obligation, as when one has lost his breviary (and cannot do it from memory), or when one is gravely ill. It is moral when, although he could absolutely speaking fulfill the obligation, it would impose upon him a grave inconvenience or torment, as when one has a severe headache, when one is agitated in spirit, or has just emerged from a soul-disturbing experience.

Q. 383. Can one who plays the organ to accompany the choral Office consider himself dispensed from its actual recitation?

A. If he, while playing, joins in the recital of the psalms and of the other parts of the Office, as if he were in the stalls, he certainly satisfies the obligation, for no one can say that the playing of the organ is incompatible with the choral routine. But if he does not join in the recital he does not satisfy the obligation. Although the playing of the organ is most compatible with the act of praying, it is still true that he who merely plays does not recite the Office. The precept is to recite the Office, not merely to pray.[22]

Q. 384. In a doubt as to whether one's illness is of a kind sufficient to excuse him from the recitation of the Office, what is to be done?

A. One should depend on the advice of the doctor or of his superior.

Q. 385. If one is sure that he cannot possibly recite the entire Office, is he held to any part of it?

A. He is held to recite that part of it which is within his power to recite.

[22] St. Alphonsus, *Moral Theology,* IV, 19.

Q. 386. If one fears that he will not be able to say the Office on the following day, is he held to anticipate on the preceding day?

A. No. Strictly speaking, the obligation runs from midnight to midnight. The anticipation of Matins and Lauds is only by privilege, and no one is obliged to use this privilege.

Q. 387. When is a mortal sin committed by failure to say the Office?

A. When it is omitted without a grave reason or without a proper dispensation. This means either the entire Office or any hour of it, or any parts of it which quantitively amount to a single hour.

Q. 388. Would the omission of Vespers on Holy Saturday constitute matter for a mortal sin?

A. Probably not, for although Vespers is an integral hour its brevity on Holy Saturday is so exceptional that it does not seem it could constitute sufficient matter for a mortal sin.

Chapter 23

The Conventual Mass

Q. *389.* What is a conventual Mass?
A. A conventual Mass is that which is celebrated in the presence of a religious community.

Q. *390.* Is there an obligation on a religious community to celebrate a conventual Mass?
A. In male religious communities which are obliged to the recitation of the Divine Office, unquestionably there is the obligation of the conventual Mass (can. 610, 2).

In female religious communities, even if they are obliged to choir, with reference to the conventual Mass, the Code says that they are to provide for its celebration "as far as it may be possible" (can. 610, 2).

Q. *391.* Is it necessary to satisfy the obligation of a conventual Mass, that the entire community assist at it?
A. That is to be recommended without doubt, yet strictly speaking, to satisfy the obligation it suffices that there be present at least four of the persons obliged to choral recitation, this number including the priest who says the Mass. The required number may be even less if the constitutions so determine it (see Q. 345).

Q. *392.* In the number necessarily required to satisfy this obligation may laybrothers and laysisters be counted?

A. No. They must be religious obliged to the choir (Sacred Congregation of Bishops and Regulars, August 6, 1858).

Q. *393.* May there be counted in that number religious with simple vows in an order whose members in due course will be advanced to solemn vows?

A. According to the ruling of the same Congregation cited in the above Question, they may be counted. As for novices, see Q. 346.

Chapter 24

The Other Practices of Piety

Q. *394.* How often, according to the Code of Canon Law, must a religious receive the sacrament of penance?

A. Canon 595, I, 3, recommends that all the religious should go to confession once a week.

Q. *395.* May superiors inquire about the observance of this recommendation, and in cases of negligence may they command its observance?

A. Yes, they may, since the Code recommends the practice. A superior can inquire if a religious is faithful in approaching the sacrament regularly, and if he discovers any negligence, he may recall his subjects to its practice. Of course, it is up to the confessor to judge the dispositions of the penitent and to regulate himself in the tribunal as he deems best.

Q. *396.* With what frequency, according to the law of the Church, are religious to be exhorted to receive Holy Communion?

A. The Code, can. 595, 2, instructs the superiors to foster among their religious subjects the frequent, and even daily reception of Holy Communion. Religious are to be left free to receive even daily if they are fittingly disposed.

It is to be noted, however, that if a religious after his latest sacramental confession has given grave scandal to the community and has committed a grave external fault, unless it is known that he has gone to confession again, the superior may lawfully forbid him to go to Communion (can. 595, 3).

Q. 397. What is to be said concerning Mass?
A. The Code enumerates among the practices of piety to be followed by religious the daily hearing of Holy Mass, though it does not impose it as a strict obligation. It charges the superiors to be vigilant on this point (can. 595, I, 2).

Q. 398. Is there an obligation of making daily the mental prayer or meditation?
A. This practice is highly recommended by the Code, can. 595, I, 2, and is generally imposed by the constitutions of each religious institute.

The Code does not determine when this should be made, or for what length of time. By custom it is not less than half an hour each day and it should be continuous for the half-hour unless some necessity demands its interruption.

Q. 399. What is meant by spiritual exercises or a retreat?
A. Spiritual exercises, or a retreat, may be defined as a period of time during which one withdraws as much as possible from ordinary occupations to devote more attention to the needs of his soul in silence, prayer, and recollection.

Q. 400. When does the Church prescribe spiritual retreats for religious?
A. They are to be made at least once a year (can. 595, I, 1).

Further, the Church prescribes them before the start of the novitiate and before taking the first vows. The retreats are to be at least eight full days in duration (can. 741; 571, 3).

Q. 401. Is there an obligation to make these spiritual retreats before the renewal of vows, and particularly when one is to make perpetual or solemn profession?

A. Abiding strictly by the letter of the Code, it seems that spiritual retreats are obligatory only before the first profession, as we have said above, Q. 240. For any succeeding profession, including the perpetual and even the solemn, it seems that there is no obligation, for the Code in speaking of any renewal of profession simply observes: "The religious profession is to be renewed in conformity with what is prescribed in the particular constitutions" (can. 576, 1).

Now whether the constitutions of any religious institute prescribe a retreat before any renewal of vows or not, it is certainly in harmony with the spirit of the Code and with the very nature of the matter that a brief spiritual retreat at least precede any renewal of vows (see Q. 240).

~~~~~~

Chapter 25

The Privileges Enjoyed by Religious

~~~~~~

Q. 402. What is meant by a privilege?
A. A privilege, in its legal meaning, is a particular law which confers a certain benefit.

It is a law inasmuch as the privilege imposes not on the privileged but on others the obligation to recognize and respect the privilege.

It is a particular law, for it embraces not a universality of persons, but a particular one, or a particular group of persons; for instance, the members of a family, the members of a confraternity, the members of a religious institute, and so on.

It confers a certain benefit to the privileged, as, for example, the granting of exemption from a tax, the right to hold office, the right to demand certain services, and so forth.

Q. 403. How many kinds of privileges are there?
A. We may distinguish privileges which are contrary to law and privileges which are outside the law.

A privilege contrary to law excuses one from an obligation

imposed by common law, as, for example, when one is excused from paying a tax imposed by law or from performing a service to which all are obliged by law.

A privilege outside of the law is one which is not in contravention to any existing law but which is granted when the law itself says nothing about it; for example, the privilege the Holy Father grants to some priests to bless rosaries imparting thereby the apostolic indulgences.

Q. 404. What is another classification of privileges?
A. Privileges may be either common or proper.

Common privileges are those which can be participated in by more persons or groups of persons who find themselves in the same circumstances; for example, the privileges which all religious have of being free of the jurisdiction of civil tribunals, as we shall see below, Q. 407.

Particular privileges are those which are expressly given to one person or to a determined category of persons without the privilege being extendible to other persons even if these find themselves in similar circumstances; for example, the privilege granted to a religious house to reserve the Blessed Sacrament not only in the principal chapel, but also in the novitiate chapel.

Q. 405. What is the privilege "of the canon"?
A. The privilege so-called of the canon consists in this, that the Church "punishes with special penalties anyone who physically injures or in any way maltreats an ecclesiastic or religious. It is called the privilege of the canon because the penalties that are inflicted on a perpetrator of any injury to a sacred person were determined for the first time in a canon or article of the Council of the Lateran held in 1139.

Q. 406. What are the penalties?
A. Whoever lays violent and guilty hands or inflicts any

physical injury on a religious incurs an excommunication reserved to the bishop (can. 2342, 4).

"Whoever" here means any man or woman, including an ecclesiastic or religious. The person, however, must be over fourteen years of age, since no censure can be incurred by anyone under that age (can. 2230).

"Lays violent hands or inflicts any physical injury" means doing corporal harm to the religious by killing, striking, or in any other way injuring the person.

"Guilty hands" means that a sin is involved in the act. Further, for the excommunication to hold, the physical injury must be sufficiently grave as to constitute a mortal sin.

Q. *407.* What is meant by the privilege "of the forum"?
A. The so-called privilege of the forum consists in this, that all ecclesiastics and religious are removed from the jurisdiction of the secular courts and may be called for judgment only before ecclesiastical courts.

The purpose of this privilege is not, as some have thought, to let go unpunished any delinquents, but since these possible delinquents are ecclesiastics or religious, it is more fitting and opportune that they be tried, and if guilty, punished by the competent ecclesiastical authority on whom they immediately depend.

The origin of this privilege is very ancient. In Catholic kingdoms it was always respected, at least up to the time of the French Revolution. Nowadays there are not many nations which honor this privilege in whole or in part.

Q. *408.* What penalties are incurred by those who violate it?
A. "If anyone cites a religious before a lay tribunal without having first received the permission of the ordinary of the place, he incurs immediately, if he is a cleric, suspension from the office he holds, reserved to the ordinary; if he be a

layman, he is punished by his own ordinary with penalties proportionate to his fault (can. 2341).

Q. 409. What is the privilege of exemption?
A. The privilege of exemption, in our case, consists in this, that by virtue of it some religious are withdrawn by will of the Holy Father from the ordinary jurisdiction of the ordinary of the place and placed immediately under the jurisdiction of the pope, or of the superior of the order to which they belong, or under other superiors appointed by the pontiff. They are therefore exempt, that is, independent in whole or in part, of the jurisdiction of the ordinary (Q. 24).

Q. 410. What is the privilege of immunity?
A. The privilege of immunity consists in this, that by virtue of the privilege religious persons are exempt from performing certain duties or obligations of the civil life.

Q. 411. How is this privilege enjoyed today?
A. According to Canon Law, by virtue of this privilege, religious:

1. would be exempt from military service and from holding any civil office which is not fitting for an ecclesiastic (cans. 12, 814);

2. would have a right to special consideration in case they are burdened heavily with debts. In this case, although they could be constrained to liquidate their debts, they should always be left that which, in the prudent judgment of the ecclesiastical judge, is strictly necessary for their living (can. 271).

In many countries today this privilege is not recognized, even in part, by the civil laws.

Chapter 26

The Right to Beg

Q. *412.* What permission must religious have in order to beg?

A. The religious strictly called mendicants, in the diocese in which they have their convent, may beg with the permission of their superior. Outside of the diocese, they must have the written permission of the ordinary of the place wherein they want to beg.

Concerning religious who are not mendicants:

1. If they are of diocesan law in order to beg publicly they need the written permission of the ordinary of the place in which their house is located, and of the ordinary of the place wherein they wish to seek alms (can. 622).

This canon of the Code advises the ordinaries of the place not to be too easy in giving these permissions to beg, particularly when there are others there whose purpose is to beg. Were it to suffice for the needs of a community, there should be no seeking of permission to beg in a diocese not their own, and they should even try to restrict themselves to a portion of their own diocese.

2. If they are of papal law they cannot publicly beg without special permission of the Holy See and without the leave, given in writing, of the ordinary of the place, unless the

privilege granted by the pope excuses them from this provision in clearest terms (can. 622, 1).

Q. 413. Who, in this last case, is the ordinary of the place? Is it the one in whose diocese the house is located or the one in whose diocese the begging is to be done?

A. According to the norm of paragraph 2 of the cited canon 622, it seems that the ordinary where the begging is to be done is meant. We read in the same paragraph that religious of diocesan law must seek the permission both of the bishop in whose diocese they have their house and of the bishop in whose diocese they wish to beg. It appears then, that religious of papal law, after they have received permission from the Holy See, which in their case takes the place of their own ordinary, are to seek the permission of the ordinary of the diocese in which they wish to beg.

Q. 414. What rules should be observed?

A. Besides the rules of prudence and of convenience, all religious who beg should observe each of the instructions which the Holy See has given or will give in reference to begging on the part of religious men and women (can. 624).

Among the principal instructions given by the Holy See and still in force as contained in a decree of the Sacred Congregation of Religious under date of November 21, 1908, are the following:

1. Begging religious shall bring with them credentials to show that they have been authorized to beg for alms. These documents are to be shown gladly whenever a pastor or bishop demands them (par. I, 6 of the above decree).

2. They shall go in pairs (*ibid.*, sec. 3). The decree makes certain exceptions to this rule, as when the begging is done in the same place in which their religious house is located or when the begging religious is well known to the public. These exceptions hold for religious men, but they do not hold for religious women. The Code recommends that reli-

gious women never go out of their house alone (can. 607). Hence, for the purpose of begging this rule is to be observed all the more.

3. In seeking alms in places far away from their convent or monastery, they shall not stay in hotels, but apply to the parish priest or other priests, or more appropriately to the religious houses in that place for hospitality in charity. If necessity forces them to accept the hospitality of a secular family, they must choose one well noted for its Christian piety and solid virtue (*ibid.*, sec. 9).

4. Religious shall not remain outside of their house for more than a month if while seeking alms they do not go beyond the limits of their diocese. If they have had to go outside of their diocese, they must not remain more than two months out of their house. Further, those who have just returned from a begging trip are not to be sent out immediately on another. They are to be kept in their house for an interval of one or two months after each trip, in proportion to their absence, and must resume the full practice of the regular life (*ibid.*, sec. 10).

5. When they seek alms in the locality of their own religious house, they must return to the house for the night, never remaining away from it overnight (*ibid.*, sec. 11).

6. Begging religious should always and everywhere reflect humility, modesty, and cleanliness; they should avoid places which are not in harmony with their vocation, and while out of their house they should faithfully practice their spiritual duties and the exercises of piety they ordinarily perform in their house (*ibid.*, sec. 12).

7. Superiors should not fail to give to the begging religious all those counsels which they believe to be necessary and prudent (*ibid.*, sec. 13).

Appendix

The Brief Dialogue
of Saint Catherine of Siena
on Consummate Perfection

As we said in the preface, we are now adding as an appendix a brief revelation on consummate perfection which is attributed to St. Catherine of Siena. We consider it a fitting crown to all the things we have said about the religious state, which is a state of perfection.

Since this little work does not come to us in its beautiful native Tuscan in which St. Catherine had dictated it to her secretaries, but in Latin, we had to select from among the many translations made from the Latin the one we thought best. That of Father Morassi, of the Order of Preachers, from the Latin text of the year 1543, seems most adequate. We have selected that one for the simple reason that, although it may not carry the thirteenth century flavor of more ancient texts, it does possess the advantage of being understandable to the kind of persons for whom this *Catechism on the Religious State* has been written.

The Dialogue

She (Catherine of Siena), having received a light from the Author of Light, came to a realization of her misery and weakness, of her ignorance and natural inclination to sin. Thereupon she began to contemplate some truths concerning the greatness of God, His wisdom, power, goodness, and all the other perfections of His divine Majesty. She saw with astonishing clarity that it is right and fitting that He should be served and honored in all His perfections and sanctity. It is right because He, being the Creator and Lord of the universe, made all things so that each in its own way might unceasingly praise His Holy Name, and that all of them should be destined to give Him glory. Particularly is it fitting, and even obligatory, that His intelligent creatures show all respect to their Lord, faithfully serve, and dutifully obey Him.

The good God was pleased to make man a rational creature, composed of body and soul, who, should he use his will well and remain a faithful servant until death, would be rewarded with eternal life, full of such joys, none of which he would otherwise be able to obtain. Few indeed are there who fulfill their duty; very few, in fact, who are saved (Matt. 7, 14). They think of their own concerns and not of those which respect Jesus Christ (Phil. 2, 21).

Catherine also saw that the life of man is very short. The hour and the moment of the terminating of his merit are most uncertain. After death, by an irrevocable and inevitable sentence, every man receives his just reward or punishment, according to the kind of life he led. In hell there is nevermore a chance of salvation. She saw also that many talked about a great number of things; that they discussed and treated in many and diverse ways the virtues by which God is to be honored and faithfully served. On the other hand, so small was the capacity of the rational creature, so darkened his intellect, so fallible his memory, that he neither could perceive many things nor retain them faithfully in his mind. Many took every care to become instructed, but there were very few who reached the perfection of actions by which God is to be served, as is our bounden duty. Therefore, almost all, disquieted by a thousand cares and tossed amid a thousand fluctuations of spirit, find themselves constantly in extreme peril of their souls.

At the sight of all these things, Catherine remained highly moved. Then, having become resolute before God, with a great desire and transport of love, she demanded insistently of the divine Majesty that He would deign to instruct her with some brief and succinct rules of perfection, and these to be so complete as to combine in themselves all the truths found in any kind of spiritual writings and in the teaching of all the Sacred Scriptures. By observing these rules one could lead a holy and perfect life, and God would be served and honored in due manner. In this way, at the end of our passage from this mortal life, so short and miserable, the eternal reward promised by God would be ours to enjoy.

And the Lord, in the manner of the holy desires which He places in one's heart and which He never fails to grant, made Himself present to Catherine's soul bringing ecstasy to her spirit, and spoke thus to her: "My beloved, your wishes prove very agreeable to Me, and they please Me in such a way that I assure you there is a great need for them to be satisfied. Since this is so, I greatly desire that you should wish them, that you should want to the full all those favors which are necessary or useful, or even only convenient for your eternal salvation. Wherefore, behold Me most disposed to please you and to satisfy your every desire. Listen, then, and put your mind on what I, the ineffable and ever infallible Truth, am going to tell you. In condescending to your demands, I will expose in brief what is the one thing which in itself so effectively crowns the sum total of all the virtues, of perfection itself and of sanctity most sublime; the one thing which comprises precisely the teachings of all the masters of the spirit and all the books of the Sacred Scriptures put together. If you mirror yourself in it and conform yourself to it, you will live constant in its practice and you will come to accomplish exactly what is both clear and obscure in the books of the saints, so as to render you worthy to enjoy from henceforth a perpetual peace and a joy, ineffable as it is eternal.

"Know, then, that the salvation of My servants and their perfection depend solely on this: *That in everything they do My divine Will.* This is to be done continuously and they are to force themselves to do it with all their might, so that in every moment of their lives all of them undertake to seek Me, to know Me alone, to please Me alone. Let them attend to this duty with the greatest diligence so that they may advance nearer to perfection. The nearer they approach Me, the closer will they be united to Me in whom most eminently all perfection resides.

"If you want to understand better this most sublime truth which I have revealed in brief words to you, pour forth your love on Him who is the object of My infinite complacency, My Son, Jesus Christ. He has emptied Himself, taking the form of a servant and making Himself like to men in all things except in sin, so that you, encompassed in darkness and wandering off the way of truth, may be given light to find your way back in the splendor of His divine light.

"Observe how My Son keeps Himself in the constant practice of an obedience unto death, precisely for the purpose of teaching you that your salvation depends on a strong and efficacious resolution to do My will alone. The person who diligently wishes to examine and meditate upon the life and doctrines of My Son will clearly see that all sanctity and perfection consist in nothing else than in the faithful, persevering submission to My will alone. Indeed, He Himself, My Beloved Son and your most loving Savior, frequently reminds you of this very truth. Recall, for example, that He said: 'Not all who say to me, Lord! Lord! shall enter into the Kingdom of Heaven, but he who doth the will of my Father' (Matt. 7, 2).

"Note that He does not repeat the word, Lord, without a definite purpose. Since all the grades of men on earth can be reduced to two general categories, namely, religious and worldlings, He desires to signify by that repetition that no one belonging to either category can arrive at eternal beatitude, though he render externally every sort of honor to Me, if he does not, at the same time, accomplish in all things My divine will.

"If you wish, then, in imitation of your Savior, perfectly to do My will on which your whole happiness depends, it is necessary indeed that in everything you reckon not your own will but that you contradict it and make it die within you. The more perfectly you do this, the more perfectly will you live in Me; and the more perfectly you purge your heart of all the personal wishes you have therein, the more abundantly will I fill it with those that are Mine."

*   *   *

The soul of Catherine, having heard these most salutary utterances of Truth, became all joyous. In her happiness, she made this rejoinder: "Oh my God, my Father, I am supremely happy, far more than I can ever express. I thank Your most amiable Majesty for what You have made me understand. I know most assuredly, as I know myself with my own little knowledge, that it cannot be otherwise than as You have revealed it to me, and have illustrated it so well by the example of my most loving Savior. Since You are the Supreme Good and all Goodness, who cannot wish sin but only that which is holy and honorable, I am resolved to do all that I ought to do for the accomplishing of Your will. This I do, even though for love of You I have to deny my own will. You never force this will of mine but leave it free. Therefore, I, in subjecting my will to Your will, become more dear to You and my merits increase before You. I greatly desire to accomplish all that You have told me, but I do not know as yet in what direction Your will points, and in what obedience I can totally consecrate myself to You. Hence, if I am not too presumptuous, if I do not abuse Your loving kindness with too great boldness, I humbly beseech You to instruct me briefly on this point which I so greatly desire to learn."

And the Lord said to her: "If you desire in a few words to know perfectly My will so that you can fully accomplish it, behold this is what it is in essence: That you love Me as much as you can and never cease to love Me; that you love Me with all your heart, with all your soul, and with all your strength. It is on the observance of this precept that all your perfection will depend, for so it is written that the 'end of the commandment is charity' (I Tim. 1, 5), and that 'love is the fulfillment of the law'" (Rom. 13, 10).

* * *

To these things Catherine replied thus: "I understand well, O Lord, that You desire my perfection, and this perfection consists in loving You. I want to love You as I ought, with a consuming love, with the most ardent charity. But in what way I should or could love You, I do not yet understand well enough. Therefore, I beg and implore You to give me more light on this point."

And God said to her: "Listen, then, and with all the attentiveness of your mind concentrate on what I am about to tell you. If you wish to love perfectly, three things are to be done:

"The first is to detach your will and completely sever it from every love that is carnal and worldly, so that in this life you love nothing that is temporal, low, or transitory. You are to love only Me. Further, and above all, that you must not love Me for yourself, or yourself for yourself, or your neighbor for yourself, but only Me, even you yourself for Me, and the neighbor for Me. Divine love cannot tolerate any other love or any other earthly affection with Itself. Whenever you permit your heart to be infected with the contagion of earthly things, you sin against My love and you lose perfection. A soul to be pure and saintly must have a disgust for all which, to the senses, might be alluring and pleasing. Never permit anything which I in goodness created for the use of man, to become an obstacle in loving Me. See to it that everything created aids you in loving Me, incites you to love Me, and inflames you with love for Me. I have created all things and I have given them unto you so that through them you may the more fully understand the greatness of My goodness, and, upon this understanding, rise to a purer love of Me. Hold courageously in check your appetites and carnal desires. By exercising a constant vigilance over yourself, you will make easier the resisting of the temptations which a corrupt nature, as well as the miserable mortal life you are living, incite in your heart, so that you too may sing with My prophet: 'Blessed be the Lord, who hath made my feet like the feet of harts, and who setteth me upon high places' (Ps. 18, 34). Your affections are the feet of your soul, which I make fleet as the hart, so that it can escape the dogs and snares of earthly concupiscences, whereupon I set thee at last in a high place, which is that of sweet contemplation.

"When you have fully accomplished all this, then you can proceed to the exercise of the second thing to be done and which is of greater perfection. It is this: Direct all your affections, all your thoughts, all your actions solely to My honor; occupy yourself constantly and with all your powers to praise Me, to glorify Me with prayers, with words and by example, and in any other manner within your capacities. Do this, so that not only you, but all around you, become inflamed with the same love and desire for Me, so that all may know Me alone, adore Me alone and love only Me. This pleases Me more than the first step, because through this more perfect love My divine will is more directly and more perfectly accomplished.

"There remains now the third step, which, when you reach it, nothing, I assure you, will be wanting to you, since you will have arrived at consummate sanctity. This is what you are seeking and steadily acquiring by forcing yourself to strengthen the disposition of your spirit to be one thing with Me, to have your will like and conformable to Mine, which is most perfect, whereupon you will not only shun evil, but even any good which I do not wish for you. Whatever happens to you in this miserable life, no matter if its nature be temporal or spiritual, should never be permitted to disturb your peace or the serenity of your spirit. Keep yourself every moment constant in the firm belief, founded on a living faith, that I, your omnipotent God, love you more than you can ever love Me, and that I exercise over you the most diligent care, far more diligent than is your concern for Me. The more perfectly you consecrate yourself to Me in the manner I have just described, the more will you abandon yourself to Me; wherefore so much the more will I comfort you with My graces and make you feel how close I am to you. Thus you will come to know increasingly better and experience more abundantly the tenderness of My love for you.

"No one can arrive at this perfection except by means of a stable, constant, and complete surrender of one's own will. If one fails to acquire this spirit of surrender, he fails to acquire this most sublime perfection. He who with a good heart surrenders his will to Me immediately, and in the highest degree does My holy will, which pleases Me; wherefore I abide in him and he in Me. There is nothing more pleasing to Me than to abide in you and to operate in you with My grace, for, 'My delight is to be with the children of men' (Prov. 8, 31); to transform them into Myself, in such a way that they become one with Me in participation of My perfection, especially of My enduring peace and of My most perfect serenity, if they so desire it, for I do not want to restrict their freedom.

"That you may the better understand how ardently I desire to possess this peace with you, and that you may be the more inflamed with a burning desire to subjugate and unite your will to Mine, think on and attentively consider this: I decreed that My Only Begotten Son should take flesh, whereby My divinity, thus despoiled of every vestige of grandeur and of glory, united itself to humanity. This great act of benevolence and of charity was done, this ineffable proof of My love was given, in order that I could entice you to draw nearer to Me and inspire you to unite your will with Mine in equal partnership, thereby remaining forever united and bound to Me. Who has desired this union more than I? I decreed that My own Son should undergo a painful, cruel, and horrifying death on the cross so that He could destroy your sin by His bitter passion—that sin which had raised a wall dividing Me from you and which had so effectively separated us that I could no longer look favorably upon you in any way. Who, again, in the greatest of the sacraments has prepared a table whereon is offered for your communion the body and blood of My own Son. It has been little prized by men, but in the eating and drinking thereof you could be transformed and changed into My very Self. As the bread and wine on which you feed change into the substance of your body, so you, by feeding yourself, under the appearance of bread and wine, on my own divine Son who is one with Me, will in spirit be transformed into Me. This is what I declared of old to my servant Augustine with these words: 'I am the food of giants; grow so by feeding on Me. You will not change Me into you, but I will change you into Myself' " (Confessions of St. Augustine).

*   *   *

When Catherine heard through these words what was the will of God and understood that to accomplish it perfectly it was necessary to have perfect charity, which could not be obtained except through a complete denial of one's will, she spoke thus to the Lord:

"You have manifested your will to me, O Lord, my God! You have told me that if I want to love You perfectly, I must love nothing that is worldly or base, not even my very self, for myself, but that I must love everything for You, and indeed only for You. You have indicated that in order to love You, I must seek in all things You alone, and praise, honor, and glorify You alone at every moment with the greatest zeal. Furthermore, I must see to it that others are inspired by me to do the same; I must force myself, likewise, to endure with tranquil mind and joyous soul every adversity which may befall me in this miserable life.

"Since I must perform all these things which You have revealed to me by the surrender of my will so that the more I die to myself the more perfectly I live in You, be pleased, I beg You, to afford me a clearer picture of my duties by instructing me in what way I can try to acquire this great virtue of the perfect denial of self."

And the Lord, who is so good, and who cannot refuse any wish of His creatures, thus replied:

"Hold as certain that every good of your life depends on the perfect denial of self. I will fill you with My grace in the measure that you empty it of your own desires. Every perfection of yours is effected precisely because of its participation in My divine goodness through the medium of grace, without which the human creature, with reference to those things which bring him his true perfection and dignity, is pure nothingness. If you truly wish to arrive at this perfection, you must prostrate yourself before Me. By a very genuine and inner conviction of your own lowliness and emptiness, you must seek always and with great care only this: to obey Me alone and do only My will. To accomplish this it is necessary that in your mind you picture your soul as a little spiritual temple constructed and completely sealed with the material of My will alone, to which you must retire to make of it your permanent dwelling. No matter where you may go physically, spiritually you will never leave its precincts; and on whatever you rest your gaze, you will see nothing of what is outside that temple. My will alone will permeate all the feelings of your soul and body in such a way that you will never speak of anything except that which you know is pleasing to Me and in accord with My will. My Holy Spirit will teach you what you shall have to do in every situation.

"There is another way by which you can arrive at the denial of your own will, namely, by having directors who can instruct and guide you according to My spirit. By submitting your will to theirs, by obeying them, following always their counsel, by entrusting yourself and all that is yours fully to them, you will be doing My will, for, 'he who heareth them (my prudent and faithful servants) heareth Me' (Luke 10, 16).

"Over and above this, I want, first, that with firm faith and profound humility you ponder that I, your most glorious God, who have created you for heavenly bliss, am eternal, supreme, and omnipotent; that I can perform for your benefit anything which pleases Me, and that there is no one who can oppose My will. No good can ever come to you except that I bestow it in accordance to what I have already declared through My prophet: 'Shall there be an evil in a city which the Lord hath not done?' (Amos 3, 6).

"Secondly, that you seriously meditate on the truth that I, your God, am the perfect intelligence, the knower of all things, the infinite wisdom; and, therefore, I see all things with utter clarity, so that in governing you, the heavens, the earth, the whole world, and the entire universe, I cannot in any way be

deceived or fall into the slightest error; for if it were otherwise, I should not be wise, nor should I be God. In order that
you may know better the depth of My infinite wisdom, understand that even from evil itself, from pain and from sin, I
know how to bring about good, a good even greater than the
evil.

"Thirdly, that you consider attentively that I, your God, am
supremely good. I am in very essence all charity and all love,
so that I cannot wish anything but those things which for you
and for everyone else are not useful and salutary. From Me
no evil can emanate; I could never wish any evil upon My
creatures. In My goodness I created man and I continue to love
him with incomparable charity.

"When you have meditated deeply and with firm faith on
these truths, you will see that the tribulations, the temptations,
the insults, the hardships, the fears, the illnesses, and all the
other adversities of your life are permitted to befall you
through My providence only unto the profit of your eternal
salvation. Through these things which you consider evil, it is
My intention that you correct your conduct by striving for
virtue, which alone can lead you to that true and supreme
good up to now unknown to you. Illumined in such a manner
by My living light of faith, you can proceed better to will your
own good. You are aware, of course, that your very knowing
of, your ability to accomplish, and your very desire for your
own good, depend entirely on My grace.

"See to it, therefore, that you submit your will to Mine in
all sincerity. By doing this, you will find lasting peace, tran-
quillity of soul and calmness of spirit in having Me forever
with you, for 'I have fixed My dwelling in peace' (Ps. 75, 2).
No thing thereafter will be able to change you, or vex you,
or be in any way a cause of scandal, or of sin, as Psalm 118,
verse 165, has it: 'Much peace have they that love thy law,
and to them there is no stumbling-block.' They love so much
My law, which is My will in the government of all things, and
they are so intimately bound to Me through it, that they find

a great delight therein, with the result that nothing except sin, which offends Me, is able to disturb them, no matter what happens to them, from whatever source or in whatever quantity or degree.

"Wherefore, having their mental eyes clear and bright, they see that from Me, the Sovereign Ruler of the Universe who governs all things in admirable wisdom, order, and love, nothing can proceed except that which is good. I exercise care over them and their affairs much better and with far greater advantage to them than they themselves know how to exercise it, to will it or to accomplish it. By considering that I, and no one else, am Author of all things that happen to them, they become strong in the possession of an unconquerable and lasting patience that permits them to suffer complacently all things that happen and, to be joyous in finding refuge in all crises in My bosom, where they taste the ineffable sweetness of My most ardent love.

"It is this which is the true 'thinking of the Lord in goodness' (Wisd. 7, 1), that is, in every tribulation and difficulty, one must believe, remember, and meditate upon the fact with pleasant and joyous spirit that I govern all things sweetly, and that everything proceeds from the inexhaustible fountain of My infinite goodness. The great benefit which results from this holy meditation and docile disposition of spirit is that nothing can prevent, corrupt, or destroy the peace of union with Me except the love of yourself for self and the pursuance of your own will.

"If you destroy in yourself the roots of self-love and self-will, there will be no hell for you, neither the one of eternal torment of the body and of the soul, which has been prepared for the damned, nor the one of internal, degrading discord which men create for themselves and which they suffer in this mortal life through their continuous solicitude and rabid lust for a thousand and one things.

"If truly you wish to live in grace in this world, which will pass, and in glory in the world which will have no end, die to yourself by surrendering and putting aside your own will. 'Blessed are the dead who die in the Lord' (Apoc. 14, 13). It is further written: 'Blessed are the poor in spirit' (Matt. 5, 3). These are they who in some manner already see Me in the course of their pilgrimage through earthly life by reciprocal love, and who later will see Me face to face in heaven in glory and happiness forever."

"So be it!"

Index